D0449318

The MUELLER REPORT

The Leaked Investigation into President Donald J. Trump and His Inner Circle *of* Con Men, Circus Clowns, and Children He Named After Himself

JASON O. GILBERT

A Very Dishonest Lightweight Who Somehow Obtained a Copy

Simon & Schuster Paperbacks
New York London Toronto Sydney New Delhi

Simon & Schuster Paperbacks
An Imprint of Simon & Schuster, Inc.
1230 Avenue of the Americas
New York, NY 10020

This book is a work of fiction. Any references to historical events, real people, or real places are used fictitiously. Other names, characters, places, and events are products of the author's imagination, and any resemblance to actual events or places or persons, living or dead, is entirely coincidental.

First Simon & Schuster trade paperback edition September 2018

For information about special discounts for bulk purchases, please contact Simon & Schuster Special Sales at 1-866-506-1949 or business@simonandschuster.com

The Simon & Schuster Speakers Bureau can bring authors to your live event. For more information or to book an event contact the Simon & Schuster Speakers Bureau at 1-866-248-3049 or visit our website at www.simonspeakers.com.

Interior design by Jason Snyder

Manufactured in the United States of America

1 3 5 7 9 10 8 6 4 2

Library of Congress Cataloging-in-Publication Data is available.

ISBN: 978-1-9821-0927-1
ISBN: 978-1-9821-0928-8 (ebook)

I joked recently about, "Can you imagine Putin sitting there waiting for a meeting and Rubio walks in and he's totally drenched?"

No, you got to have Trump walk into that meeting, folks, we'll do very nicely. We're going to do very nicely.

—Presidential nominee Donald J. Trump, February 26, 2016

About the Typefaces Used in the Mueller Report

As a tribute to the subjects of this report, we have used several new typefaces throughout.

The bulk of the text is written in **MAKE HELVETICA GREAT AGAIN**, a sans serif font that is as easy to read on a baseball cap as it is on an indictment for obstruction of justice.

Portions have also been rendered in the **FAILING TIMES NEW ROMAN**. This Times New Roman is in no way failing; indeed, it is thriving. The designer contributed this font on the condition of anonymity, fearing retribution from the Trump White House.

Finally, many of the media reports have been printed in **SERIF HUCKABEE SANDERS**. Can you trust anything written in Serif Huckabee Sanders? Probably not. But, hey, it's your only choice.

CONTENTS

INTRODUCTION

To the American People:

I am the leaker of the report you are about to read.

While I cannot divulge my true identity, I am someone who sees the President every morning and night; who has known the President for the past two decades; and who is present for many of his tantrums, outbursts, and extended rants about Chuck Schumer.

I can't say my full name, for it might jeopardize my relationship with the President.

And so: call me only "Melania T."

I had been saying for years that I wished Donald Trump was in prison. And so when I heard that Special Counsel Robert Mueller had been appointed to investigate President Trump, I knew immediately that I wanted to help. But how?

I had much to offer, given my proximity to Donald. Would Mr. Mueller want the President's credit card statements from the Moscow airport Sbarro? Would he want an exceptional amount of hair from his shower drain? What about a recording of the President discussing Russia with his two most trusted advisors: Geraldo Rivera and Chumlee from *Pawn Stars*?

I contacted Mr. Mueller—again, using only my pseudonym, Melania T.—and became his investigation's secret source: the Deep Throat of the Mueller investigation.

At first, my spycraft turned up nothing. I recovered the President's legal pad from a meeting with the White House Commission on Science and Technology, but it only contained a crude stick figure drawing of Bo Derek with the phrase "Time travel?"

Next, I recovered his notes following a cabinet meeting about the Iran deal. This, too, proved a bust, as his notes were just a list of ideas for nicknames to call Keith Olbermann on Twitter.

For several months I turned up nothing of use for Mr. Mueller, even though the President had become quite careless. On a trip to Asia he attempted to order an adults-only pay-per-view to his hotel television but instead of calling the front desk, he left a voice mail for Glenn Thrush at the *New York Times*.

For three confusing minutes in September 2017 the President accidentally appointed Scott Baio as chief justice of the Supreme Court. In October 2017 the President hung up on the prime minister of Australia after he refused to "hand over his country's secret recipe for the Bloomin' Onion."

"I thought we were *ALLIES*!" the President screamed, slamming down the receiver.

But I refused to give up. We have a saying in my native Slovenia: "It is the persistent and cunning wolf who catches the strutting, spray-tanned chicken."

And by God did I want to catch that chicken.

So I kept funneling information to Mr. Mueller. I had full access to the White House since the President was never there on weekends. I forwarded documents left in printers, and Filet O' Fish wrappers, and receipts for $19 iced teas from the Trump International Hotel Bar & Grill.

I was also able to record many of the President's conversations by hiding a tape recorder in the binder that carried the President's Daily Briefing—which, luckily, the President never opened.

And then one night in the summer of 2018 I was in the President's bedroom and I had a hunch that something was up.

The President had been in an irritable mood; that morning he had accidentally retweeted seven accounts that all turned out to be either neo-Nazis or Piers Morgan. The *Washington Post* had run a story showing his average approval rating was somewhere in between gas station empanadas and the ending of *Lost*. He had been lashing out all day, and he could not even be cheered up by his nightly phone call in which Sean Hannity soothingly sings "You Are My Sunshine."

I received my signal from Mr. Mueller: a text message that read "DEEP STATE." The President was fast asleep, which I can always tell because he was sleep-talking about "fake news Wolf Blitzer."

Just to be extra sure, I said out loud, "Honey! Jeff Bezos is here. He wants to apologize for pretending to have more money than you and for generally being an inferior businessman."

But he did not move. That meant he was out cold.

I had to sneak out of the White House without anyone knowing. Luckily the President had fired the longtime chief of White House security and replaced him with a 23-year-old Trump supporter whose previous security experience was checking IDs at a T.G.I. Friday's in Whitefish, Montana.

I tiptoed through the halls of the White House. It was around midnight; I saw no one except for Stephen Miller, wearing a cloak and reciting a German poem to a portrait of Andrew Jackson. He did not notice as I crept by him, out into the night.

I met Mr. Mueller at our usual spot, a place we knew that no one in the Trump administration would ever visit: the National Museum of African American History and Culture.

Mr. Mueller told me he suspected that he would soon be fired, and that if he was, he wanted to get something out into the world. He handed me the following documents and gave me instructions to put it in the hands of a writer that no one was interested in: not the FBI, not the CIA, not any readers.

I googled "unemployed writer + no prospects + looks like he cuts his own hair" and the first four pages of results all pointed to Jason O. Gilbert. I thank him for shepherding this report into the world and hope that he soon purchases some clothing that does not feature visible Cholula stains.

As you will see, the documents are mostly raw materials: interview transcripts, meeting notes, emails, and other communications filed into evidence by Robert Mueller and his team of investigators. Due to Mr. Mueller's worries about imminent termination, the report is in no way comprehensive.

Disappointingly, the report does not reach a conclusion about criminal activities of either Mr. Trump, his associates, or his children. I will not state one, either. Though I am an expert on many subjects—fake smiling while holding hands in public with someone you dislike; feigning interest in stories about going to Studio 54 with Roy Cohn—collusion is not one of them.

Still, I hope you will read these documents and draw your own conclusions. Mr. Mueller and I have risked much to bring you this report. But take it from someone who has watched the President attempt to launch preemptive military action against an episode of *Jimmy Kimmel Live!*: the risk of inaction is much greater.

Be Best,
"Melania T."

Part One

The FIRING *of* JAMES COMEY

Interview with President Donald J. Trump (Portion)

Oval Office, July 10, 2018

Despite several defiant tweets to the contrary, President Trump readily agreed to be interviewed under oath, with no conditions about what we could ask him. The following represents a portion of that interview, conducted in the Oval Office in May 2018.

Q: What was your first contact with the Russians?

TRUMP: It would have been 1987. I was in the VIP lounge at Lou Ferrigno's pool party. All the heavy hitters were there: Don Johnson, Lee Iacocca, ALF, the little Amish boy from *Witness*, two of the three California Raisins. This beautiful woman named Anya—she was Miss Minsk 1984—comes straight up to me and whispers in my ear—Anya! Is Anya here? Come on up here, Anya!

Q: Mr. President, it's just you and me in the Oval Office.

TRUMP: Anyway, Anya and I hit the jacuzzi with Olivia Newton-John, Mayor Ed Koch, and an Irishman we later discovered wasn't Bono, and—

Q: President Trump, do you know why I'm here?

TRUMP: Am I giving you a medal?

Q: No.

TRUMP: Are you giving me a medal?

Q: President Trump, you are under investigation for collusion and obstruction of justice.

TRUMP: Wait, seriously? Did you not not see my tweets where I called this a witch hunt?

Q: Our first series of questions concerns the dismissal of FBI Director James Comey.

TRUMP: Okay, but let me state for the record that this phony investigation is an excuse by the Democrats to distract from our administration's tremendous accomplishments. You know, the other day Tim Cook—CEO of Apple, very successful—visited the White House and he said to me, "Mr. President, the Fake News Media will never admit this but you're making Abraham Lincoln look like a chimpanzee riding a bicycle."

Q: Tim Cook said that?

TRUMP: And I thought those were very strong words, and so true.

Q: Are you ready to begin, President Trump?

TRUMP: Absolutely. But before we start, may I just state one more thing for the record?

Q: Sure, feel free to say anything you—

TRUMP: WITCH HUNT!!

A *Politico* Playbook Newsletter About James Comey's Upcoming Senate Testimony

May 2, 2017, Seven Days Before James Comey Gets Fired

In early May, James Comey was preparing to deliver testimony to the Senate regarding the FBI's ongoing investigation into Russian meddling in the 2016 election. The following POLITICO Playbook newsletter suggests that President Trump was attempting to influence that testimony.

POLITICOPLAYBOOK

DRIVING THE DAY

COMEY TESTIMONY DAY LOOMS: Trump Trembling as FBI Director Prepares to Testify—45 Looks to Persuade Comey—STAY COOL: D.C.'s Hottest Look Is Once Again Pleated Khakis—FIRST IN PLAYBOOK: Willie Geist Got a Haircut—BIRTHDAY: Mercedes Schlapp's Miniature Poodle Turns Seven

FIRST UP: Trump's team is nervous about what Comey might say at his Senate Judiciary Committee hearing tomorrow. "The guy could sink us," one source says via AIM.

4 THINGS TO LOOK FOR: Comey could: 1) indicate that the probe is winding down, 2) indicate that the probe is heating up, 3) contract a rare virus that puts the country in danger, or 4) reveal he's leaving the FBI to open a tea parlor called James Comey's Jams & Sconies.

STAY SMART: Once you buy coffee from Starbucks, you can take home as many napkins as you want.

*******A MESSAGE FROM THE COMPANY FORMERLY KNOWN AS BLACKWATER:** We know we screwed up. But if you get a bad haircut, do you stop getting haircuts for the rest of your life? Hire us to lock down Pakistan or you will regret it. That's a threat. **www.BackInBlackwater.com** *****

PARTY TIME: Sean Hannity celebrated his ratings at L'Ambassadeur with Tucker Carlson, Wolf Blitzer, Senator Ted Cruz (R-TX), Senator Dianne Feinstein (D-CA), Susan Sarandon, George Soros, the mysterious fifth Koch brother, Loretta Lynch, the dog from *Air Bud*, Brendan Dassey, the kids from *Stranger Things*, a performance by A$AP Mob, and astromech droid BB-8.

SPOTTED: The deputy spokesperson for Kansas senator Jerry Moran ordering a chicken ciabatta sandwich at Au Bon Pain . . . Mike Huckabee playing a banjo for no one at an empty bus station . . . Ali Velshi crashing his bicycle into an SUV parked in the bike lane on MacArthur Blvd. (h/t Newt Gingrich) . . . Newt Gingrich parking his SUV in the bike lane on MacArthur Blvd. (h/t Ali Velshi).

NEWS FLASH: Chemical waste lobbying firm Krasten Horowitz Lederman Fernandez has hired EPA director Scott Pruitt as SVP of Policy. Pruitt will remain EPA director . . .

WATCH OUT: It's another beautiful day outside. . . .

LOOK ALIVE: I haven't eaten a meal with another person in 14 months. . . .

STAY FRESH: My closest friends say that writing this newsletter has rotted my social skills and made me unlikable. . . .

KEEP COOL: My girlfriend Julie left me because I "was starting all my sentences with unnecessary two-word exclamations." . . .

BIG NEWS: Carly Fiorina spotted eating cream of mushroom soup alone at a T.G.I. Friday's . . .

WHAT'S NEXT: Expect Team Trump to ramp up the charm offensive on Comey prior to his hearing. PLAYBOOK is hearing that something is going down tonight at Mar-A-Lago . . .

The 2017 Donald J. Trump Awards for Achievements in Tremendous Friendship and Loyalty to Donald J. Trump

May 2, 2017, 8 p.m.

The day before Comey's Senate testimony, President Trump threw a private awards gala at Mar-A-Lago: "The Donald J. Trump Awards for Achievements in Tremendous Friendship and Loyalty to Donald J. Trump." Most viewed this as a transparent attempt to send a message to James Comey on the day before his testimony.

Here is the full transcript of President Trump's opening monologue.

Ladies and gentlemen, good evening, and welcome to the Donald J. Trump Awards for Achievements in Friendship and Loyalty to Donald J. Trump.

I am your host, Donald J. Trump. I know we all have a lot of work to do except for me, so I'll keep these remarks short.

The movies have given us many depictions of loyal and tremendous friends in unforgettable duos like Thelma and Louise, Buzz Lightyear and Woody Harrelson, and Tom Hanks and the decapitated head of his friend Wilson in *Cast Away*.

I am happy to say that the winner of this year's prize has shown tremendous friendship and loyalty to Donald J. Trump, and I am hopeful that he will continue to do so in the coming years, in the coming weeks, and in any upcoming appearances he may have in front of the Senate Intelligence Committee.

This year's prize—which includes a gorgeous statuette in the mold of Tawny Kitaen and a $10,000 check courtesy of our friends in the Qatari government—goes to FBI Director James Comey.

Now, James couldn't be here tonight, because he is, by sheer coincidence, preparing to testify tomorrow. But I know he is watching, both because he was so excited to win the prize and because I had the NSA hack his phone so that the livestream would appear on his home screen no matter what.

James Comey reminds me of a story I once heard while I was aboard my friend Jimmy the Snake's sex yacht. Forgive me if you've heard this story before; I did recently tell it to the Boy Scouts.

So, Jimmy the Snake is a wonderful guy, a real family man, always there to lend an ear or a tire iron. I used to attend these crazy parties he would throw on his boat, and there would be girls and booze and women and girls. This was a simpler time, of course; this was two months ago.

Anyway, I'm in the Hose-Down Cabin and I'm getting briefed on Iranian chemical weapons by General Buzzkill, or whatever the bald guy's name is, and Jimmy the Snake walks in. He says, "Donald, I've got a problem. Your guy James Comey is trying to arrest me on bogus charges of racketeering, tax evasion, credit card fraud, drug smuggling, conspiracy to assassinate a racehorse, purchasing biblical artifacts from ISIS, and unlawful ownership of a military tank. You're not gonna turn on me, are you, Donny?"

And I looked Jimmy the Snake right in the eye and said, "No way, Jimmy. Because I am a tremendous friend, and loyal, and that's not what tremendous loyal friends do."

I told this story to my Tremendous and Loyal Friend James Comey and he didn't think it was funny.

But I don't consider James Comey a tremendous and loyal friend because he laughs at my jokes; he's never been a guy to fake a smile or accept a box of stolen Applebee's gift cards.

He's a real friend. And real friends stick by each other; they don't go blabbing in front of the Senate Intelligence Committee. Otherwise he will forfeit this beautiful Tawny Kitaen statuette—not to mention my tremendous, loyal friendship.

All right, everyone. We're gonna take a quick break, and then we'll be back with the stand-up comedy stylings of Commerce Secretary Wilbur Ross. Let's have a good time tonight!

Conversation between President Trump, Reince Priebus, Steve Bannon, and Jared Kushner

May 2, 2017, 8:30 P.M.

Later that night, President Trump fretted with aides Reince Priebus, Steve Bannon, and Jared Kushner about whether Comey had received his message. The president's wife was also nearby, holding a giant bouquet of flowers that she pointed toward their conversation.

TRUMP: What do you think? Did that do the trick?

REINCE PRIEBUS: It was a *wunderbar* speech. Lincoln-esque.

TRUMP: Town Car or Navigator?

STEVE BANNON: Sir, as the Greek philosopher Epicharmus once wrote, "He who inhabits the mindset of the warrior shall crumble if he should not prevail over blind wisdom."

TRUMP: Steve, I have no idea what you just said, you're at a black-tie gala wearing a cargo jacket, and you smell like a microwave that's exclusively used to reheat salmon.

BANNON: You want my opinion? Fire them. Fire all of them.

TRUMP: All of who? Comey's people?

BANNON: Don't stop there. Fire every last government employee. The FBI. The CDC. Postal workers delivering their globalist propaganda Babies 'R' Us catalogs.

KUSHNER: Oh God, here we go.

BANNON: The "government" is a failed social convention that has distracted man from his true nature: to live naked out in the barren plains and wrestle grizzlies for food. We need to burn it all down with a cleansing—

KUSHNER: "With a cleansing fire that unleashes the true potential of American braun." We've heard this speech before.

TRUMP: Let's just hope Comey's on board. I'm gonna hit the shrimp buffet; someone get Steve a bow tie and a gallon of Trump cologne.

Text Messages Re: Donald J. Trump Awards

Much later that night, President Trump received the following text messages from his personal attorney, Michael Cohen.

Michael Cohen

Hi Don.

How are you?

Donny.

Are u there?

Okay

I'm gonna say it.

I saw that you gave out trophies called the Donald J. Trump Awards for Loyalty and Friendship

I am a bit offended that I did not win one.

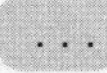

Haha

Just kidding

Do you want to go fishing this weekend?

Let me know.

Btw “operation darken stormy” is complete. Hush agreement signed

No one will ever hear about it

Unless she gets some kind of attention-seeking lawyer

Who finds a way to wriggle out of it

And is on Anderson Cooper 360 like every night for a month

Not gonna happen

Also if I won a DJT for Friendship and Loyalty at a separate ceremony, like how the oscars do technical awards, i understand

Anyway

Thanks.

See you soon!

Haha sorry i’ve had a couple drinks

All right, good ngiht man

Senate Testimony of James Comey

May 3, 2017, Six Days Until James Comey Gets Fired

The following is a relevant snippet of testimony from James Comey that may have gotten him fired. It was found printed out in Trump attorney Michael Cohen's apartment with the handwritten message "OVER THE LINE!" followed by Mr. Trump's signature.

SENATOR RICHARD BURR: Director, do you have any doubt that the Russians attempted to collude with the Trump campaign?

FBI DIRECTOR JAMES COMEY: None.

BURR: And is it your opinion that we have more to learn about this collusion attempt, Director?

COMEY: It is, Senator.

BURR: And, Director, is it possible that your investigation might uncover other crimes in the Trump family unrelated to collusion?

COMEY: I'm afraid I can't answer that question in an open setting, Senator.

BURR: Are there specific Trump family members you are investigating?

COMEY: Again, I can't answer that question in an open setting, Senator.

BURR: Okay, but what if I triple-donkey dared you?

COMEY: Are you triple-donkey daring me, Senator? Or are you asking what would happen if you hypothetically triple-donkey dared me?

BURR: I triple-donkey dare you to answer the question, Director Comey.

COMEY: Triple-donkey dare, no take-backs, no finger-crossies, no loosey-goosies?

BURR: Cross your heart, hope to die, shoot a pistol in your thigh, Mr. Director.

COMEY: Very well. In that case: We would be looking to uncover crimes in the Trump family unrelated to collusion.

BURR: Based on what, Director Comey?

COMEY [*gesturing vaguely*]: Everything.

BURR: I will yield the remainder of my time to Senator Rubio, who I believe has some more questions about Andrew McCabe's wife's purchase of a political bumper sticker in 2002.

Email from Devin Nunes

Meanwhile, Congressman Devin Nunes kept the White House up to date on his own investigation into the 2016 election.

FROM: **Devin.Nunes8@aol.com**

TO: **JaredKushner@WhiteHouse.gov**

SUBJECT: **Major Breakthrough in Investigation**

Hey man,

I know today seems rough for the President, but I have some great news about my ongoing 9000-page investigation into Russian collusion.

I've chosen a font.

It's *COMIC SANS*.

Would an official investigation into Russian collusion use *COMIC SANS* if it was going to find the President liable for a crime?

Checkmate, Libs,

Devin Nunes

—Sent via the AOL™ Mail™ app on my Verizon™ Motorola™ Droid™ 3—

President Trump's Complaint List

May 5, 2017, Four Days Until James Comey Gets Fired

The next day, Chief of Staff Reince Priebus sent one of his regular emails to the White House staff. The email suggests that President Trump was preparing to fire FBI director Comey due to his Senate testimony.

FROM: **Reince.Priebus@WhiteHouse.gov**

TO: **AllStaff@WhiteHouse.gov**

SUBJECT: **President Trump's Complaint List for Week of 05/05/2017**

Hello Staff,

I hope you are having a *Wunderbar* day! First of all, I have baked an entire tray of *streusselkuchen*—a traditional pastry from my home *stadt* of Wisconsin—and I have placed them in the break room. Make sure to sprinkle on some of the *Apfelzucker*!

I wanted to let you know that President Trump will not be working this weekend, starting Wednesday at 11AM and running through Monday or Tuesday, depending on the condition of the greens at Trump National–Bedminster.

But the primary reason for this communication is that this week's COMPLAINT LIST is here! These are President Trump's biggest gripes, in precise bulleted list format. Let's all think about how we might improve ourselves the following week, *ja*?

16. The Oval Office is not currently equipped to deep-fry funnel cakes.

15. The president wants a walkie-talkie. Doesn't matter who's on the other end, just as long as he can carry around a walkie-talkie.

14. Yesterday Eric Trump visited the president at the White House. He never should have made it past the front gate. What happened?

13. The Department of Veterans Affairs is nowhere near as sexy as its name indicates.

12. The White House should have "a beautiful elevator, with big tremendous gold buttons, like you would see at a Gimbel's department store in the '40s."

11. Someone keeps deleting Twitter from the president's phone. If you are going to play a prank on the president by deleting something from the president's phone, please make it Eric's contact information.

10. The president is not to be disturbed, for any reason, when he hangs a Domino's Pizza delivery bag on his door handle

9. Sean Spicer's suits fit like "a garbage bag draped over a corn dog."

8. We're beginning to think that up to 35 percent of the protesters in the Women's March were anti-Trump.

7. Why doesn't the White House have its own cheerleading squad?

6. Why doesn't the White House have a monorail?

5. Why doesn't the White House offer subprime mortgages for first-time home buyers?

4. Why doesn't the White House have a dungeon?

3. Why hasn't the White House bowling alley been equipped to offer Cosmic Bowling?

2. Why is "Cosmic" only offered at bowling alleys? We should offer a "Cosmic White House Tour" and "Cosmic Intelligence Briefings."

1. James Comey has to go.

Google Searches of President Donald J. Trump

May 6, 2017, Three Days Until James Comey Gets Fired

President Trump began to lay the groundwork for FBI director Comey's dismissal. The president conducted the following searches on Google from his Oval Office computer.

Google

"Can i fire someone for being taller than me"

"Can i fire someone because i don't like seeing his face"

"Obstruction of justice how do we legalize it"

"Can the president trade an employee like a baseball player"

"Would James Comey for Ichiro be a fair trade?"

"How much to hire david blaine"

"David blaine can make person disappear?"

"David blaine disappearing trick does it kill the person?"

"Can the president appoint an fbi SUPERdirector"

"Dog the bounty hunter is he employed?"

"Dog the bounty hunter interested in fbi superdirector?"

"Fbi director why do we even need it"

"Like what would happen if we just didn't have an fbi director"

"IHOP pancake delivery washington d.c. area"

"Is stephen miller standing right behind me"

Yahoo Answers Post by President Donald J. Trump

After finding little help on Google, President Trump turned to one of his closest White House advisors: Yahoo Answers. He submitted the following question later that day.

YAHOO! ANSWERS

Politics & Government | Politics | Donald J. Trump | Legal Help

Let's say Strong Negotiator President Donald J. Trump wanted to fire Ungrateful and Disloyal FBI Director James Comey. How would he do that without getting into legal trouble?

Asked by: PresTrump45454545

Best Answer: You would need to get a memo from AG Sessions or Deputy AG Rod Rosenstein explaining why you need to fire him. That will give you legal cover. —Virgil F.

OTHER ANSWERS

- The poster has no idea what he is talking about. The president can go ahead and fire Comey. Does not need to provide a reason. "Virgil F." is probably a 14-year-old boy who has never seen a boob. —Tommy P.

- Um I can assure you I'm not a 14-year-old boy and I have seen plenty of boobs, including your mom's. Are you Jewish? —Virgil F.

- BUILD THE WALL AND ARREST ANTIFA LEADER BERNIE SANDERS —TrumpTrainMaga Q.

- Ready to earn extra cash?? $$$$ I make $475/day from the comfort of my own home!!!! Visit MasterMoneyCash.biz today and start earning REAL money today! —Ruslan M.

- Bernie Sanders would have defeated Hillary Clinton if not for the meddling of Debbie Wasserman-Schultz in the DNC Primary. A recent blog post by Glenn Greenwald proves that we should

---

—End of relevant portion of website—

Rosenstein and Sessions Discuss the James Comey Firing Memo

May 8, 2017, One Day Until James Comey Gets Fired

On May 8, President Trump decided to fire James Comey. The following conversation between Attorney General Jeff Sessions and Deputy Attorney General Rod Rosenstein occurred in a nondescript hallway at an unspecified time of day. The conversation was recorded and forwarded to our office by Melania T.

SESSIONS: I've just met with the president. He's decided to fire James Comey and he'd like you to write a memo explaining why.

ROSENSTEIN: Okay. Why are we firing Comey?

SESSIONS: That's what the president is asking you to explain.

ROSENSTEIN: So what's the explanation?

SESSIONS: The explanation is the president wants to fire James Comey.

ROSENSTEIN: So why doesn't he just fire Comey?

SESSIONS: Because he needs a memo explaining why.

ROSENSTEIN: And why does he need a memo?

SESSIONS: He needs the memo to fire Comey.

ROSENSTEIN: But why is he firing Comey?

SESSIONS: That's what he wants you to put in the memo.

ROSENSTEIN: Wants me to put what in the memo?

SESSIONS: The reason why he's firing Comey.

ROSENSTEIN: Which is what?

SESSIONS: That's for you to put in the memo.

ROSENSTEIN: I don't understand.

SESSIONS: Just write in the memo why we must fire James Comey.

ROSENSTEIN: Okay.

SESSIONS: Because the president wants to fire Comey.

ROSENSTEIN: Okay.

SESSIONS: Because without an explanation for why the president is firing Comey, the president can't fire Comey.

ROSENSTEIN: Okay.

SESSIONS: Okay.

ROSENSTEIN: Okay.

SESSIONS: Okay.

ROSENSTEIN: Do you ever get the sense that there is no explanation for any event in this White House, that we are governed only by chaos, and that our every action originates from some absurd entropy that no just God would possibly countenance?

SESSIONS: No.

ROSENSTEIN: Okay.

SESSIONS: Okay.

ROSENSTEIN: I'm going to write the memo now.

They do not move.

A Memo from Deputy Attorney General Rod Rosenstein Explaining Why James Comey Is Being Fired

May 9, 2017

On this day James Comey was fired. Rod Rosenstein wrote the memo laying out the reasons for his dismissal, reprinted below.

Office of the Attorney General
Washington, D. C. 20530

President Donald J. Trump
The White House
Washington, DC, 20500

Dear President Trump,

Webster's defines "unqualified" as "not officially recognized as a practitioner of a particular profession or activity through having satisfied the relevant conditions or requirements."

I think we can all agree that this succinct and clear definition applies to our current FBI director, James Comey. He has proven himself to be not only unqualified, but unsuitable, unsuited, ill-suited, ill-prepared, unlicensed, and a (colloquial) quack.

I could go into the many reasons why we have reached this determination, but I do not wish to bore you, Mr. President. I'm sure we're all thinking about a million different specific events that make James Comey unqualified. That unfortunate occurrence in 2014; his unacceptable behavior at that function (I think it was in Utah?) in 2015; and, of course, his total lapse of judgment as it pertains to the controversy with the guy with the mustache in 2016.

Suffice to say that there are events, ugly events, which definitely exist, that we are all aware of.

For these reasons, I recommend that you remove Mr. Comey from his post and identify new leadership for the FBI. America needs a director who is qualified, suitable, suited, prepared, licensed, and, most importantly, not quack.

I hope this is enough?

Sincerely,

Rod Rosenstein
Deputy Attorney General

Email from Chief of Staff Reince Priebus to the White House Communications Team

May 9, 2017

Following Director Comey's firing, the White House initiated a communications strategy intended to deflect attention away from the FBI's Russia investigation. An email from Chief of Staff Priebus to the White House communications team makes this clear.

FROM: **Reince.Priebus@WhiteHouse.gov**

TO: **AllComms@WhiteHouse.gov**

SUBJECT: **Trump Spin Team: Assemble!**

Hello my talking heads!

I spoke with President Trump and he would like us to engage in a media blitzkrieg to get in front of this impending Comey *Scheissesturm*.

He wants you to get out onto as many television programs as possible and defend him against these nonsense allegations that he fired James Comey to obstruct the Russia probe. He wants us to be like Chris Pratt when a *Guardians of the Galaxy* movie comes out: totally omnipresent and completely unavoidable.

Your only guideline: if you are asked why the president fired James Comey, *do not* mention the Russia investigation. I will leave it up to you all to agree on an alibi; so long as Russia is not mentioned, we are fine with it.

Okay, *danke*, and we'll see you on the small screen! Can't wait to see what you come up with!

Reince

Person of Interest: **Kellyanne Conway**

Kellyanne Conway, seen here telling NBC's Chuck Todd that the president has never even met Billy Bush.

ROLES: Counselor to the President; Frequent Appearances on CNN, MSNBC, and Fox News; Even More Frequent Appearances on PolitiFact's "Five-Pinocchio Pants-on-Fire Lie of the Week"

FORMER ROLES: Author of the best-selling 2014 book *How Republicans Can Win in 2016 Without Bashing Immigrants or Nominating a Serial Adulterer Who Is Frequently Humiliated on The Howard Stern Show*

SKILLS: Possesses an encyclopedic knowledge of historical massacres that never happened

ACCOMPLISHMENTS: Once made it through an entire segment of *Face the Nation* without starting a sentence with "What the President was clearly *trying to* say was . . ."

FUN FACT: UCLA scientists once converted the outrage she produces during a normal television appearance into electricity that powered a small town in Nevada

Counselor to the President Kellyanne Conway's Appearance on *The Lead with Jake Tapper*

May 10, 2017

The publicity blitz after Comey's firing began almost immediately.

JAKE TAPPER: We're joined by Kellyanne Conway, Counselor to the President. Let's get right into it: Why did the president fire James Comey?

KELLYANNE CONWAY: President Trump did not fire James Comey. James Comey voluntarily quit in order to pursue a career in professional basketball.

TAPPER: I'm sorry? Several of your colleagues say Comey was fired, as does Mr. Comey himself.

CONWAY: Opinions can differ, facts can differ. But one thing is certain: James Comey was practicing three-pointers instead of investigating Hillary Clinton, and he was telling people he had a tryout with the Portland Trail Blazers. He left President Trump with no choice.

TAPPER: Mrs. Conway, I expect the truth from everyone I interview. So I will ask again: Why did President Trump fire James Comey?

CONWAY: Jake, the Constitution grants the president certain powers: the Power to Declare Nap Time; the Power to Convene a Celebrity Golf Tournament with Kato Kaelin and Mikey from *Growing Pains*—

TAPPER: No one is questioning President Trump's *right* to fire people.

CONWAY: Well, good. Because he has the right to fire anyone. He could fire you if he wanted to.

TAPPER: *(cross-talk)* Now, that's ridiculous, President Trump could not fire me—

CONWAY: *(cross-talk)* He could make one phone call and you'd be blogging from Salon.com!

—End of Relevant Portion of Transcript—

Daily Press Briefing with Press Secretary Sean Spicer

May 11, 2017

The next day, Press Secretary Sean Spicer delivered a press briefing where he was asked directly why President Trump fired the FBI director. A direct transcription from C-SPAN follows.

JIM ACOSTA (CNN): Sean, we still don't have an answer as to why President Trump fired FBI Director Comey.

SPICER: Jim, the president has be-cleared himself on this issue.

JIM ACOSTA: He's what?

SPICER: The president has be-cleared himself perpeatedly, Jim.

JIM ACOSTA: I don't recognize two of those words.

SPICER: Again and again the president has be-cleared himself on this fissure, and the American people recognizant of that.

ASHLEY PARKER (*WaPo*): Was that the end of the sentence? "The American people recognizant of that"?

SPICER: That was the, yes, the president has—look, President Trimp is be-cleared of all wrongdone, in the final esteem of millions of blue-working Americans of who voted.

MICHAEL BENDER (*WSJ*): Did you say "President Trimp"?

SPICER: I don't know how I can say it any clearer: Prednisent Blump has terpetually be-cleared himself on the batters disconcerting Jams Clommy. He sequestered Director Clommy for his designation and when Clommy repulsed, he had no choice but to perminate him on the commendation of Dippity Attorney Dangerbull Rob Rosenstone. Does that answer your question?

ACOSTA: Are you feeling okay?

SPICER: I'm terrific. Next question. Jonas Colvin, Breitbart.

COLVIN: Hell yes, two-part question. First: How is the President so amazing? Second: Will he sign my hat?

—End of Relevant Portion of Transcript—

A List of Personnel Who Have Left the White House and the Reasons for Their Departures

PERSON: Rex Tillerson

ROLE: Secretary of State

REASON FOR LEAVING: Insisted on playing 1940s cowboy country music on the White House Sonos

PERSON: Steve Bannon

ROLE: Counselor to the President

REASON FOR LEAVING: Landed the titular role in the 2019 live-action film *The Mucinex Man Attacks Tokyo*

PERSON: Hope Hicks

ROLE: Communications Director

REASON FOR LEAVING: Wanted to explore opportunities to serve a megalomaniac in a toxic environment in the private sector

PERSON: Gary Cohn

ROLE: Chief Economic Advisor

REASON FOR LEAVING: Realized he could make 18,000 percent more money working for Goldman Sachs

PERSON: David Shulkin

ROLE: Secretary of Veterans Affairs

REASON FOR LEAVING: Pushed back on the President's idea to open the country's first combination VA hospital/dog-racing track

---

PERSON: Omarosa Manigault-Newman

ROLE: Aide to the President

REASON FOR LEAVING: Okay, first of all, you can't fire her, because SHE QUITS

PERSON: Tom Price

ROLE: Secretary of Health and Human Services

REASON FOR LEAVING: Chartered a $98,000 private jet to pick up Chick-fil-A drive-thru

---

PERSON: H. R. McMaster

ROLE: National Security Advisor

REASON FOR LEAVING: Reunion tour with his college punk band H. R. McMaster & the Master Blasters from Planet Disaster

PERSON: Sebastian Gorka

ROLE: Deputy Assistant to the President

REASON FOR LEAVING: After discovering Gorka's troubling links to anti-Semitic groups and radical anti-Muslim views, the White House did nothing and Gorka left for a totally unrelated reason

---

PERSON: Anthony Scaramucci

ROLE: Communications Director

REASON FOR LEAVING: Thrown out by White House bouncers after getting too lit on the dance floor

---

PERSON: Sean Spicer

ROLE: Press Secretary

REASON FOR LEAVING: After running the most successful communications operation in American history, Spicer resigned as the most respected and brilliant press secretary this country has ever seen

PERSON: Vivek Murthy

ROLE: Surgeon General

REASON FOR LEAVING: Refused to reclassify the Pizza Hut P'Zone as a vegetable

---

PERSON: Reince Priebus

ROLE: White House Chief of Staff

REASON FOR LEAVING: Turned out to be a German radio DJ who applied for the job as a prank

An Email from Alex Jones, Under Consideration for Press Secretary

May 11, 2017

Apparently unsatisfied by Sean Spicer's performance, President Trump began his search for a replacement. One candidate, the InfoWars founder and supplement salesman Alex Jones, submitted the following application for the job.

FROM: **Alex.Jones@infowars.com**

TO: **Trump@Trump.com**

SUBJECT: **Comey Advice**

Hello Mr. President,

Alex Jones from InfoWars here. Thank you again for considering me for press secretary. I watched Spicer's shtick today; you could sense his beta energy emanating through the television set. He's like a human chemtrail of weakness and cuckoldry.

You're in a crisis here, Mr. President. Not as bad as the crisis of Democrats dumping estrogen into our public schools' water supply, but a crisis nonetheless.

I've put together a few talking points that I would use when dealing with the press—whether I was speaking to fake MSM publications like the New York Times or to genuine news sources like www.SwampPundit.bitcoin. This should give you a pretty good idea of how I would conduct myself as press secretary:

Talking Points Re: The James Comey Firing

• The President absolutely has the right to fire anyone.

• James Comey was being criticized by Democrats and Republicans alike.

• What's more, James Comey is a central figure in a Satanic sex cult that operates out of a Dave & Busters in Rockland County, Maryland.

• We strongly believe, based on evidence coming from the Internet, that James Comey hatched from an egg.

• If you look closely at photos of James Comey you will see that he has a forked tongue.

• Suspiciously, James Comey refused to give an InfoWars reporting team samples of either his blood or his urine when we showed up at his grandson's soccer game and shouted at him through a megaphone.

• James Comey has to buy specialized khakis from Dockers to hide his prehensile tail.

• We cannot risk the Executive Branch being overrun by Reptilian Humanoids who may be intent on impregnating us with their alien seed.

• It has been theorized that in the Reptilian Humanoid species, as in seahorses, it is the males who become pregnant.

• If you are a red-blooded American man who does not want to labor through 24 months of painful and slimy reptile pregnancy, you must support the President in his dismissal of James Comey.

You can take or leave these talking points, Mr. President. But I guarantee that if you run with these bad boys, *no one* will be talking about Russia or obstruction of justice anymore.

Alex Jones

Evidence File #3916-A

A Letter from the Portland Trail Blazers Confirming That FBI Director James Comey Did Not Have a Tryout Scheduled

September 4, 2017

Hello SPECIAL PROSECUTOR ROBERT MUELLER,

Thank you for your press request regarding A TEAM TRYOUT FOR FORMER FBI DIRECTOR JAMES COMEY. We can confirm that Mr. Comey did not have a tryout with the team, nor had he ever contacted the Trail Blazers regarding an open roster spot as a three-point specialist.

We hope this helps, and Gooooooooo Blazers!

Sincerely,
The Press Office of the Portland Trail Blazers

Trump Cabinet Members' Comments on James Comey's Dismissal

Our team of investigators interviewed several Trump cabinet members to get more insight on why Trump believed he had to fire James Comey.

MIKE PENCE (VP): I remember where I was when the president decided he wanted to fire James Comey. I was doing what I usually do: standing in a room with forty-eight other men who look and dress identical to me.

REX TILLERSON (STATE): I was sitting in the back of my pickup truck eating a rack of barbecue ribs. The Chief of Staff told us to get back to the White House for a meeting. I immediately asked if I could DJ the meeting, because I had discovered some new tunes from Billy "the Yodeling Cowboy" Haines. The Chief of Staff said this was a "No Music" meeting, so I knew it was serious.

RYAN ZINKE (INTERIOR): President Trump was hoppin' mad. When he walked in the room, he banged his knee against a filing cabinet, so he fired the filing cabinet. A White House page came in and wheeled the thing out. I heard they put it in one of the empty cells at Guantanamo.

SCOTT PRUITT (EPA): Keeping James Comey on the payroll was an unconscionable waste of taxpayer dollars.

KELLYANNE CONWAY (COUNSELOR TO THE PRESIDENT): James Comey had an indoor basketball court constructed within the FBI building, and he spent public funds to hire Scottie Pippen as a personal trainer.

TOM PRICE (HHS): We tried to cheer up President Trump. I personally bought him a taxpayer-funded charter jet to Hilton Head, down there in South Carolina? But he said he was in no mood to fly. I didn't want to let a good charter plane go to waste so I ended up using the jet like thirty-seven times over the next month.

RICK PERRY (ENERGY): The president said he had an announcement to make. For some reason I thought he was going to say that he was getting bar mitzvahed. So I shouted, as loud as I possibly could, "MAZEL TOV!" Everyone was staring at me so I got up and left the meeting.

STEVEN MNUCHIN (TREASURY): I was out of town on an official government trip to Turks & Caicos. I am sorry I missed the meeting but Louise and I were doing important government research vis-à-vis strawberry margaritas at a swim-up pool bar.

IVANKA TRUMP (??? TO THE PRESIDENT): I don't remember much about that meeting, but I do remember that I was wearing a lavender cotton tunic ($79.99) and our striped wide-leg cropped pant ($89.99). Hey, is it possible to get a hyperlink to our web store in your report?

NIKKI HALEY (AMBASSADOR TO THE UN): A bunch of us tried to talk the president out of firing Comey. We figured Comey was better than his replacement—who we all assumed was Hulk Hogan, since he was sitting next to the president in a tank top that said "I'm the Next FBI Director, Brother."

HULK HOGAN (SIX-TIME WWF WORLD CHAMPION): That was a total coincidence; I had bought that shirt years ago at a Ron Jon Surf Shop in Daytona Beach. Hell, I was just surprised that I got security clearance to sit in on an all-staff meeting with the president.

JOHN WESTERHOFF (HEAD OF WHITE HOUSE SECURITY): We do not know how Hulk Hogan was able to sit in on this meeting. An investigation is under way.

JOHN KELLY (HOMELAND SECURITY): I tried to save Comey. I told the president that the FBI did not have the authority to bring charges due to the Fourteenth Bill of Amendment Government Act of 1973. I thought that would work; lying usually works.

JAMES MATTIS (DEFENSE): Hell, even now, when Trump gets upset about your probe, we lie and tell him you aren't real. I'll say, "Mr. President, Robert Mueller is a figure from an ancient Nordic folk tale who lures naughty children into his magical fjord and then bakes them into cocktail meatballs." And then we can get back to health-care reform.

WILBUR ROSS (COMMERCE): I was asleep during the meeting. I think I might fall asleep right now. What time is it? Hey, if I start snoring, don't steal my wallet?

ELAINE CHAO (TRANSPORTATION): I don't think the president knows who I am. Every time he sees me he congratulates me for winning a different collegiate sports title. "Hey there, you must be on the UNC lacrosse team. Great work!" "Villanova men's basketball. NICE!"

BETSY DEVOS (EDUCATION): Why did the president fire James Comey? That might be one of those questions we never learn the answer to, like “How many continents are there?” or “Was Napoleon real?”

KELLYANNE CONWAY: At the end of the day, the president is the president because he is the president. And James Comey was fired because he entered the NBA Draft.

MIKE PENCE: This President will always make the decision that will benefit the American people and that will speed forth the Judgment Day where God returns to earth to punish the wicked in a glorious rapture of hellfire and doom.

STEVE BANNON (WHITE HOUSE CHIEF STRATEGIST): Mike Pence said *what*?

REX TILLERSON: Hey, has anyone seen Ben Carson? He hasn’t shown up for work in like three weeks.

Evidence File 3812-M

Text Messages from Ben Carson Regarding the Firing of James Comey

Ben Carson, the Secretary of Housing and Urban Development, was the only cabinet member not to attend the meeting, as his assistant said that he was "on one of his nightly walks through the aisles of a Rite Aid."

While I did not question Mr. Carson about James Comey, the following text message conversation was forwarded to our office. The texts were sent between Secretary Carson and a man whom he believed was President Trump but was, in fact, a Lyft driver named Gary who had driven Mr. Carson the night before.

Ben

Hello, Mr. President. I want to assure you during this Comey drama that you have my full and total support

He was not up to the task, Sir

Gary

This is not the President

This is Gary, from Lyft

White Toyota Corolla

Ben

Mr. president, this is Ben Carson

Your Secretary of Housing and Urkel Development

Urkel Development

Urkel

I can't get my phone to stop typing Urkel

U R B A N

There we go: Secretary of Housing and Urkel Development

Dammit

Gary

Again, this is Gary from Lyft

Did you forget something in the car

Ben

Donald, this is Ben Carson

We did the debate together

I was a doctor once

Or maybe a dentist

They made a movie about me

Called "Garfield: A Tail of Two Kitties"

Gary

If you left something in the car I can drop it off for you for $10

Ben

Now that you mention it

I think I left my seat belt in the car

Gary

That's my seat belt

It's part of the car

Ben

I'm pretty sure I brought my own seat belt

Mr. president

Is the government off for National Pancake Day?

[30 minutes later]

Okay

Thank you Mr. president

See you at the next cabinet party

Another Update from Devin Nunes on His Congressional Investigation

Meanwhile, Congressman Devin Nunes submitted another update to his ongoing counterinvestigation into Russian collusion.

FROM: **Devin.Nunes8@aol.com**

TO: **Jared.Kushner@WhiteHouse.gov**

SUBJECT: **Another Update**

Hey Jared,

I know the blowback from the Comey firing looks rough, but I've got some great news. I got some explosive information from a well-placed source (I can't say who it is). Don't want to spoil it all, but . . .

Six words: James Comey hatched from an egg.

More soon, my brother.

Devin Nunes

—Sent via the AOL™ Mail™ app on my Verizon™ Motorola™ Droid™ 3—

Person of Interest: **James Comey**

Former FBI Director James Comey, seen here at the 2017 Axios Public Integrity Summit Sponsored by Theranos

ROLE: FBI Director under Barack Obama and Donald Trump; Best-selling Author of *A Higher Loyalty* (as James Comey) and *The Girl with the Dragon Tattoo* (as Stieg Larsson)

FORMER ROLE: Tall Guy Standing in Front of You at Neil Young Concert

SKILLS: Posting Instagram photos of the sunset with captions like "Thinking about when our Founders acted with integrity. . ."

ACCOMPLISHMENTS: Tipped his high school election to the bully who was running as a joke after pointing out that the more qualified candidate "didn't follow hallway postering protocol"

FUN FACT: Appeared on a 1984 episode of *Star Search* as one-half of break-dancing crew Comey and the Snake

WHAT WE'RE LOOKING INTO: Whether President Trump attempted to obstruct justice in the Russia probe by firing Mr. Comey

Interview with Former FBI Director James Comey

Because of my prior friendship with former FBI Director James Comey, I am sharing the full transcript of our conversation, lest I be accused of favoritism.

I met with Mr. Comey at his home in Virginia. He had succeeded me as FBI director under President Obama in 2013. I had heard that he was working on a book; I assumed, knowing James, that it was either a history of chalk or a guide to properly maintaining the cleanliness of one's tennis shoes.

It was difficult to contain my enthusiasm upon meeting with a dear old friend. I was immediately transported back to our wild heyday at the FBI: looking through manila folders, sipping coffee, placing the manilla folders back in their appropriate places.

We were no longer those wild young bucks, of course. And I can assure you that as an investigator, I was 100 percent professional, even if my excitement occasionally leaked through.

MUELLER: Mr. Comey, thank you for meeting with me.

COMEY: The pleasure is mine.

MUELLER: I am very happy to see you.

COMEY: Joy is coursing through my veins.

MUELLER: Enough with the frivolities. Mr. Comey, why do you think the president fired you?

COMEY: I don't think of myself as a difficult person. I enjoy the hobbies of a typical government official living in suburban Virginia: manicuring my lawn, alerting the managers at Whole

Foods to faulty shopping carts, flossing my teeth, and, after an appropriate interval, gargling with mouthwash.

MUELLER: The dream.

COMEY: Which is to say I do not think my demeanor to be the reason for my termination. Everything I have to say about the matter I included in my memos. You have my memos?

MUELLER: I do.

COMEY: And how did you find them?

MUELLER: Impeccably typed and rigorously formatted.

COMEY: That is the kindest thing anyone has ever said to me.

Evidence File #1843-H

James Comey Memos

What follows are my notes after meeting President Trump at Trump Tower on January 7, 2017. I jotted these down immediately after leaving Trump Tower and buying a lamb gyro (lettuce, tomato, cucumber, white sauce) from a halal cart.

I have tried to recreate dialogue as best as I could remember it.

My First Meeting with President Trump

The first time I met the President was following a staff meeting. Mr. Trump had not yet been inaugurated.

The President discussed his goals for his first year in office, which he had written on a whiteboard. They included "State of the Union beats *CSI: Miami* in ratings" and "Give Presidential Medal of Freedom to Mike Ditka."

After the meeting the President ordered everyone to leave the room except "the CEO of the FBI." The room cleared. I attempted to hide behind a curtain, but I am a 6'8" man and the President was staring right at me.

"Why are you behind a curtain?" the President asked.

"I'm not," I replied.

There were five minutes of silence as the President stared at the curtain, confused. The President then walked to his desk and pushed a button. "Can you send in Comey, chief executive of the FBI?" the President said.

I stepped out from behind the curtain. "I'm here, Mr. President," I said.

The President stood very close to me.

"I need your loyalty," he said.

"I will be loyal to the Constitution," I replied.

"You mean the boat?" the President asked.

"What boat?" I said.

"The Constitution. It's a boat," the President said.

"I meant the founding document," I said.

The President thought about this.

"I once made love to a Miami Dolphins cheerleader on Carl Icahn's boat," he finally said.

I did not know how to reply, so I turned to leave. The President grabbed my shoulder. He had the slim fingers of a waifish French child.

"I need your loyalty," he said again. "I need you to triple-pinky swear that you will be loyal only to me."

The President stuck out his tiny little pinky. It was like a genie had put a curse on a Q-tip. I pushed it away.

"No loyalty?" the President asked.

"I will always give you my honest opinion," I said.

"Then I will give you my honest opinion," the President said. "I was disappointed that episodes of *American Gladiators* didn't end with a fight to the death inside a Colosseum. I mean, 'Gladiators' is right there in the title."

That was the end of my first meeting with President Trump.

My Second Meeting with President Trump

The second time I talked to President Trump, we ate dinner together in the Green Room of the White House. I was extremely reluctant to meet with the President one-on-one, given his previous requests for loyalty and weird comments about *American Gladiators*.

"Why don't we dine with our families?" I proposed.

"I think I just lost my appetite," the President said.

It was just the two of us eating in the Green Room at the White House. We were served by navy stewards who President Trump had made dress like Grimace and the Hamburglar. The waiters placed down a big plate of spaghetti and meatballs.

"Do you want to do Lady and the Trump?" the President said. I could not tell whether he was joking, as he was neither smiling nor frowning, so I went to the restroom.

When I returned 45 seconds later the entire plate of spaghetti and meatballs had been eaten.

Mr. Trump said he wanted to talk. We spoke on many subjects; the conversation jumped around unpredictably, like a cat chasing a laser pointer.

President Trump did most of the talking and listening to him was akin to a museum tour of his brain. Topics included the 1984 Chrysler LeBaron; the marital status of Heather Locklear; whether it would be possible to open a Smithsonian Hotel & Casino; what Jake Tapper's "deal" was; Nobel Prize categories he felt he might win; whether I thought space aliens existed, and if so, whether they "liked to party."

Suddenly, the conversation shifted where I hoped it would not.

The President wanted to know what I thought of "this whole golden-showers mess." He asked if the FBI had a "Jason Bourne guy" who could "parachute into Russia" and "prove that the tape does not exist." I remarked that it would be difficult to prove that something did not exist.

"I would just hate it if this lovely woman, the love of my life, thought I did that disgusting thing," the President said.

"I can talk to Melania," I offered.

"I meant Ivanka," the President said.

Later in the dinner the President asked if I would put out a statement clearing him of "the golden cloud" over his head. I asked him not to use the phrase "golden cloud" ever again. I then said that it would be inappropriate for me to clear him in the middle of an investigation. He handed me a sheet of paper with a statement already typed up. It read:

> *This is Comey speaking. I have served as Chief Executive of the FBI for the past 67 years and in those 5 decades I have never met a man as innocent or entrepreneurial as Big Infrastructure President Donald J. Trump, King of America and Defeater of Lazy Chuck Schumer.*
>
> *It is my expert opinion, having reviewed Files and Looked through Binoculars, that the Golden Showers tape does not exist and that it is part of a FRAUDULENT DOSSIER drummed up by Sore Loser Hillary "EMAILS" Clinton to explain her historic and boneheaded loss in the election. Mr. Trump is a Great Patriot and I would certainly live in one of his beautifully appointed condos in Trump Tower–Chicago, on sale now to both citizens and noncitizens.*
>
> *It is my recommendation that we shut down the Russia investigation and move those resources to the full prosecution of real criminals, like Chuck Todd and the cast of* Hamilton.
>
> *Let us move past these petty squabbles and begin a bipartisan era of cooperation where we give Mr. Trump whatever he wants, including all of Michael Bloomberg's money.*
>
> *Sincerely,*
> *Comey, CEO of the FBI*

I told the President I would not put my name on the statement. The President growled. The dinner was clearly over.

I said good night to the President and he shook my hand. It was like shaking the hand of a Muppet Baby. That ended my second meeting with the President.

My Third Meeting with President Trump

I went to the Oval Office at 4 p.m. today for what COS Reince Priebus called a "meet-and-greet" with President Trump. I suspected that the President wanted to discuss Michael Flynn, whom President Trump had recently fired and who was now a target of our investigation.

Mr. Priebus assured me that Mr. Trump in no way would discuss the Flynn investigation. He said the President "was new to D.C. and wanted to ask if I had a good barber, my favorite ice cream shop, things of that nature." When I turned to ask a follow-up question, Mr. Priebus had vanished.

I sensed that I was being ambushed. Nonetheless I entered the Oval Office and found President Trump alone, typing something on his phone. I felt my own phone buzz in my pocket. It was a tweet from President Trump that read:

> *Meeting with Can't-Take-a-Hint Comey today. Will ask him to let up on General Flynn (Hero!) and Members of Trump family. Comey must drop investigation—or else. (Remember AMERICAN GLADIATORS!!!)*

I sat down across from President Trump. Before I could say hello, he began talking.

"I hope you can make this Flynn investigation go away," Mr. Trump said. "He's a good guy: always retweets me, comes to my improv shows, offered tons of great suggestions about policies toward Ukraine."

I agreed that Mike Flynn was a good guy but said nothing more.

"What are you doing this weekend?" the President asked.

I started to explain that my wife and I were planning to take a canoe trip but the President interrupted me.

"Maybe you should cancel those plans and also cancel the investigation into Mike Flynn," he said.

I said I was very much looking forward to my canoe trip and said nothing more.

"You know, Comey," the President said, leaning forward. "If you find a way to drop this Flynn thing, I could make life sweeter than honey for you. Whatever you want, it's yours: A top-of-the-line Toyota Supra, a VIP table at the Rainbow Room, you name it. You ever smoke an authentic Cuban cigar with Tim Allen at Bobby Van's?"

I replied that I had not. I told the President that the FBI would investigate any case it received to its conclusion and that justice would be served.

The President put his phone to his ear, even though it clearly had not rung.

"President speaking? Oh, hello, Stephen Hawking, yes I do have time to help you with math," he said into the receiver. He motioned for me to leave with a gesture of the shrunken little kitten's paw he calls a hand. The President then received an actual phone call, which I noticed was from Pat Sajak.

I exited the room. As I left I heard the President say, "Patty, baby, I haven't made a decision on a Comey replacement, but you're at the top of the list, and that's my final answer."

That was my last meeting with the President.

Interview with James Comey (Cont'd)

MUELLER: One month later you were testifying before the Senate.

COMEY: I got some excellent, intelligent questions, and I also got questions from Marco Rubio.

MUELLER: Six days after that you were fired. Did you hear anything from the president immediately following your testimony?

COMEY: I received a text message from Mr. Trump at the beginning of my testimony that read "BIG ratings for you right now; push TRUMP GOLF MEMBERSHIPS." I never responded.

MUELLER: After the Senate testimony, did you feel that you were about to be terminated?

COMEY: I saw hints. Breitbart started styling my name as ☠☠☠ James Comey ☠☠☠. One night I woke up at around 4 a.m. and Steven Miller was on my front lawn holding a Tiki torch and a scythe; when he saw me, he shouted, "Your end is nigh, Deep State!" The next day I was fired.

MUELLER: The writing was on the wall.

COMEY: And very much in the *New York Times*.

A *New York Times* Story About the Firing of James Comey, Three Days Before It Happened

May 4, 2017

This is the New York Times *article referenced by Mr. Comey, published three days before he was fired.*

Alone and Cornered, Trump Lashes Out and Considers Changes

By Maggie Haberman and Glenn Thrush

WASHINGTON—President Trump stomped around the White House, howling like a moose. He flung a bowl of hot chowder at the head of Steven Mnuchin. He sat alone in the darkness, screaming at a replay of *Morning Joe* and firing golf balls through a portrait of Rutherford B. Hayes.

The reason for his anger? FBI Director James Comey.

Following damning testimony by Mr. Comey in front of the Senate, President Trump lashed out this weekend and is in one of the worst moods of his fledgling presidency.

This is according to interviews with more than three dozen Trump associates, confidants, hangers-on, tie manufacturers, and White House pastry chefs.

He has been described as "irate," "rattled," "roiled," and "discomfited." At a staff meeting Wednesday morning, several cabinet members wore bicycle helmets in order to protect themselves from flying coffee mugs.

"The President is madder than Ancient Greek ruler Perdiccas II of Macedon," said one anonymous Trump advisor. "This country needs a street warrior to fight the globalist hordes, not a Tasmanian devil who I watched stress-eat four pounds of lasagna."

The dark cloud hanging over Mr. Trump's increasingly sweaty head comes from Mr. Comey's ongoing investigation into whether the President's campaign colluded with Russian officials. The President has called the investigation "FAKE NEWS," a "WITCH HUNT," "TOTAL NONSENSE," and "WORSE THAN CHUCK TODD!"

During recent Senate testimony, Mr. Comey confirmed that there was "at least one U.S. person or persons" being investigated but would not say whether the President was one of them. Mr. Comey also declined to say whether he considered the President a "true friend" or "just some guy he knows from work who is all right, I guess."

Insiders say that the President is close to firing Mr. Comey. He has already drawn up a short list of potential replacements for FBI director: former New York City mayor Rudolph Giuliani; son-in-law Jared Kushner; *Timecop* star Jean-Claude Van Damme; Alexander Morris, Mr. Trump's loyal and longtime dry cleaner in midtown Manhattan; Mega Man, from the video game *Mega Man*; *Wheel of Fortune* host Pat Sajak; and Brody Callaway, a twenty-one-year-old Trump campaign volunteer who has no federal law enforcement experience and who was recently arrested for public intoxication at a Chuck E. Cheese's.

"The President simply hasn't meshed with Mr. Comey," one aide said. "If the President is going to work with someone he doesn't like, it's going to be his son Eric."

White House spokeswoman Sarah Huckabee Sanders pushed back on the idea that the President was unhappy.

"President Trump is in a jolly mood and has been skipping around the White House, handing out lollipops to good boys and girls, and lighting up rooms with his radiant smile," Sanders said. "Mr. Trump has no plans to fire James Comey, doesn't know how to golf, and has never eaten fast food in his life."

Still, the mood at the White House is charged, insiders say, and they expect an explosion—one that may just blow up the tenure of James Comey as FBI director.

"If I'm Lying James Comey, who's a real lowlife, by the way," one anonymous source who is close to the President said, "I'm packing my desk. Believe me, it's so true."

Interview with James Comey (Cont'd)

MUELLER: I have one final question for you, Mr. Comey.

COMEY: Already? It's only been eleven hours of intense questioning.

MUELLER: Time flies when you're testifying under oath.

COMEY: Well then, I hope we can do this again soon. Surely the vice president has committed some kind of federal crime; the guy sounds like a televangelist soliciting donations for his church to build a spaceship.

MUELLER: In your final estimation: Why do you think President Trump fired you?

COMEY: I live my life by certain codes. Code One: Always do what's right. Code Two: If you write a book, don't make a big deal of the book tour; keep it low-key. Code Three: Never speculate about another man's intentions, no matter how obvious they may seem based on a truly incredible amount of evidence.

MUELLER: Thank you, Mr. Comey.

Interview with Donald J. Trump (Portion)

Q: So you maintain that firing James Comey had nothing to do with his investigation into you or your dealings with Russia?

TRUMP: James Comey failed me, he failed the American people, and he failed to capture the international criminal Carmen Sandiego, despite very strong resources poured into finding where in the world she is.

Q: The 2017 Donald J. Trump Awards for Tremendous Loyalty and Friendship—how did you come up with that idea?

TRUMP: No one had ever done anything like it before, but everybody said it was a tremendous awards show, better than the Highly Biased and Disrespectful ESPYs. We wrote the speeches quickly, me and Stephen Miller, a lovely guy who is so strong on both immigration and Third Reich memorabilia.

Q: This was actually the second time you held a ceremony for the Donald J. Trump Awards for Tremendous Loyalty and Friendship, correct?

TRUMP: Who told you that? Was it "Melania T."? If I ever find out who that is—

Q: You also held a gala in 2013, correct?

TRUMP: I'd like to take a recess, your honor!

Q: After you returned from Moscow?

TRUMP: WITCH HUNT! Fake News! Jim Acosta! Totally dishonest . . .This phony investigation is . . . RECORD SOYBEAN IMPORTS! Witch hunt! Witch hunt! WITCH HUNT!!!

The 2013 Donald J. Trump Awards for Tremendous Friendship and Loyalty to Donald J. Trump

On December 18, 2013, Donald J. Trump threw an awards gala at Mar-A-Lago. Melania T. forwarded us a VHS copy of the ceremony. A full transcript of Mr. Trump's opening monologue:

Hello, ladies and gentlemen! My name is Donald J. Trump and it is wonderful to be at an awards show that isn't the Emmys—who, by the way, keep on giving my award to the very untalented Jeff Probst, a weak and irrelevant guy who has never once fired Meat Loaf.

The winner of this year's award has shown tremendous friendship and loyalty to Donald J. Trump; and I hope he continues to do so in any upcoming situations where he might be tempted to leak an incriminating video that he may or may not have taken from a waterproof surveillance camera installed in the Presidential Suite at the Ritz-Carlton Moscow.

Ladies and gentlemen, I give you the inaugural winner of the Donald J. Trump Award for Tremendous Friendship and Loyalty to Donald J. Trump: he's a strong leader, he's a rugged outdoorsman, and he is hopefully very discreet about what financial information he shares with U.S. investigators—

Vladimir, you shirtless horseback-ridin' son of a gun, come on up here!

Part Two

MEETINGS *with* *the* RUSSIANS

Associates of President Trump's Campaign Who Communicated with Russian Ambassador Sergei Kislyak

Assembled by our team, this is the definitive list of all members of the Trump orbit who either communicated with or claimed to communicate with Russian ambassador Sergei Kislyak.

---

1. Jeff Sessions met with Kislyak on several occasions but did not mention these meetings during his confirmation hearings for attorney general.

2. Jared Kushner met with Kislyak about establishing a secret backchannel between Russia and the United States and did not mention this meeting on any of the two hundred revisions to his security clearance requests.

3. Michael Flynn spoke on the phone with Kislyak during the transition and made promises about what would happen when Trump became president. He also warned Kislyak about chemtrails.

4. Eric Trump claimed to be "basically best friends" with Kislyak and said that they "used to play hockey together." We have investigated these claims and he was just looking for attention.

5. Rick Perry told our investigators he had held a lengthy conversation with Kislyak but it turns out he had confused Kislyak with the actor Jon Voight.

The remainder of our investigation into Russian meetings will focus on Jeff Sessions, Jared Kushner, and Michael Flynn.

Person of Interest: **Attorney General Jeff Sessions**

Attorney General Jeff Sessions, seen here announcing his opposition to the Beyoncé Super Bowl halftime show.

ROLE: Attorney General; Trump Transition Team Member; Lead Banjo in Conservative Jam Band, White-Spread Panic

FORMER ROLES: Senator from Alabama; Pirate #3 in the 1987 production of *Peter Pan* at the Huntsville Playhouse & Gun Range

SKILLS: Hootin'; hollerin'; establishin' mandatory minimums

NOTABLE ACCOMPLISHMENTS: Recusing himself from both the Russia investigation and modern views on race

FUN FACT: Voted by his high school as "Most Likely to Be Reincarnated as a Vengeful Leprechaun"

WHAT WE'RE LOOKING INTO: Why Sessions failed to disclose several meetings with Russian ambassador Sergei Kislyak during the campaign

Text Messages Between Jeff Sessions and Senior Aide Rick Dearborn, Fifteen Minutes Before Sessions's Confirmation Hearing

January 10, 2017

In early January, then-Senator Jeff Sessions testified before the Senate Judiciary Committee as part of his confirmation hearings to become attorney general. It was later revealed that Sessions neglected to mention several meetings with the Russian ambassador Sergei Kislyak during this testimony.

This text message exchange between Sessions and his senior aide occurred fifteen minutes before Sessions took the stand. It may explain why Sessions did not bring up meetings with Russian ambassador Kislyak.

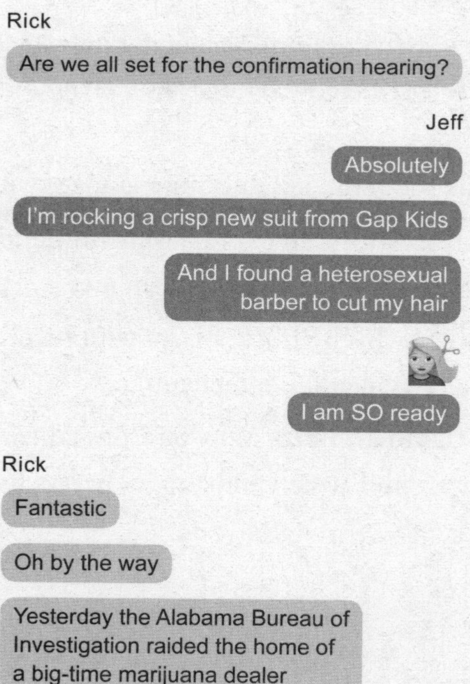

Rick
Are we all set for the confirmation hearing?
Jeff
Absolutely
I'm rocking a crisp new suit from Gap Kids
And I found a heterosexual barber to cut my hair
I am SO ready
Rick
Fantastic
Oh by the way
Yesterday the Alabama Bureau of Investigation raided the home of a big-time marijuana dealer

We shipped up the contraband to show how strong you'll be on drug enforcement

Eight pounds of marijuana, a liter of CBD oil, a bunch of edible marijuana products

Speaking of: Did you grab some Chick-fil-A or something?

You know you get cranky when you're hungry

Jeff

Yeah someone got us a tray of Brownies from Evidence Bakery

I was feeling a little nervous and I stress-ate like 3 of those bad boys

Rick

Wait . . . A tray?
From Evidence Bakery?

Jeff

Yeah, there's a table of Brownies here that says "EVIDENCE"

Cute name for a bakery near the Department of Justice imo

There was even a little sign next to it that said "Confiscated from the Scene of the Crime"

Funny right?

You should have seen me wolf down those bad boys lol

Rick

Oh, Jesus.

Senate Testimony of Attorney General Jeff Sessions

January 10, 2017

Fifteen minutes later, Senator Sessions appeared before the Senate. A relevant snippet of his testimony follows.

SENATOR PATRICK LEAHY (VT): Senator Sessions, we are approaching hour three of your testimony, so I'll keep my questions short.

JEFF SESSIONS: Isn't it weird, man, that both time and people can be short? Like, we don't measure time in inches, and we don't measure height in minutes. Did you ever think about that?

LEAHY: Mr. Sessions, did you meet with any Russian nationals during your time on the Donald Trump campaign?

SESSIONS: What do you mean by "meet"? Like, did I shake their hand? Did I become soul mates with a Russian ambassador? We can't ever really "know" another person. We put up these walls and—does anyone want Jack in the Box?

LEAHY: To be clear—you are testifying that you never met with any representative of the Russian government either during the campaign or during the transition?

SESSIONS: Back off, man. I said I didn't. Hey, isn't is crazy that the plural is *attorneys general*? If I'm confirmed, would the plural of my name be Jeffs Session?

LEAHY: I yield the floor to Senator Lindsey Graham.

SESSIONS: Lindsey, what's up, man? You wanna blow this square convention and go watch some Rick and Morty?

Text Messages Between Jeff Sessions and Senior Aide Rick Dearborn, Fifteen Minutes After Sessions's Confirmation Hearing

After the hearing, Jeff Sessions debriefed with his senior aide Rick Dearborn. Our forensic analysis shows that Sessions sent these messages from the drive-thru lane at a Taco Bell.

Jeff

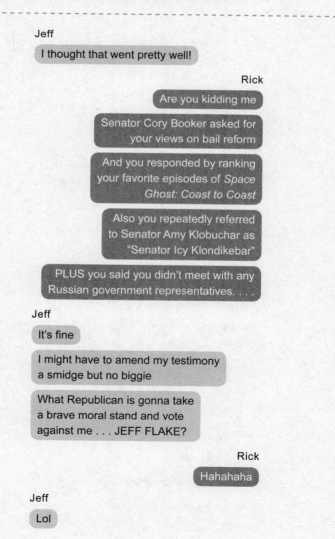

I thought that went pretty well!

Rick

Are you kidding me

Senator Cory Booker asked for your views on bail reform

And you responded by ranking your favorite episodes of *Space Ghost: Coast to Coast*

Also you repeatedly referred to Senator Amy Klobuchar as "Senator Icy Klondikebar"

PLUS you said you didn't meet with any Russian government representatives. . . .

Jeff

It's fine

I might have to amend my testimony a smidge but no biggie

What Republican is gonna take a brave moral stand and vote against me . . . JEFF FLAKE?

Rick

Hahahaha

Jeff

Lol

Text Messages Between Donald J. Trump and His Personal Physician, Dr. Harold Bornstein

President Trump received the following text messages from his personal physician, Dr. Harold Bornstein, immediately after the Sessions hearing. Coincidentally these text messages were also sent from the drive-thru lane of a Taco Bell.

Maybe: Harold Bornstein

Hey, Donny

I caught the testimony of that Jeff Sessions cat the other day

I know he's up for attorney general but i'm thinking he'd be a better fit for Agriculture

If you catch my drift

Anyway I'm taking the Winnebago up to Vermont for an open-air Crosby Stills Nash & Young concert on Joaquin Phoenix's hemp farm

And I was hoping you could put me in touch with Jeff Sessions' "sherpa"

I'm in the market for some of that "Sweet Home Alabama"

Donny?

Okay bad time

I'll see you for your "physical" in a week

Don't worry, I already entered in your weight at 239

Amended Senate Testimony of Jeff Sessions

In early 2017, now–Attorney General Sessions was forced to quietly amend his testimony after a tipster informed the FBI that Sessions had communicated with Russian ambassador Sergei Kislyak at least once.

It turns out, in fact, Sessions failed to mention several meetings with the ambassador, as he revealed in his amended testimony submitted to the Senate Judiciary Committee.

Department of Justice

November 25, 2017

To the esteemed members
of the Senate Judiciary Committee:

This is a difficult letter to write, but it appears that I may have made a misstatement or two during my testimony. Specifically, I testified that "I did not have communications with Russians during the campaign."

This is not totally accurate. I can now recall communications I had with the Russian ambassador at the time of the campaign.

Upon further review of my calendar, I met twice with Russian ambassador Sergei Kislyak in March 2016, following campaign events, where we shook hands and exchanged pleasantries. These encounters slipped my mind.

During one of these encounters, I agreed to spend a diplomatic afternoon with the Russian ambassador at Six Flags Over Biloxi. We ate shaved ice and rode the Double Dragon roller coaster three times in a row. Sergei won a giant Minions stuffed animal at the shooting gallery and we got a caricature drawn where Sergei and I were a figure-skating pairs team.

This encounter also slipped my mind.

I can now recall that as we were riding the Ferris wheel, looking out over the Biloxi skyline, I confessed to Kislyak that I always wanted to attend summer camp but hadn't had the chance. The Russian ambassador pointed out that I wasn't getting any younger.

We pinky-swore and that night the two of us enrolled at Camp Blue Star in North Carolina. I do not know how, during my Senate testimony, I failed to remember this eight-week sleepaway camp where Sergei Kislyak and I were bunk mates. Nerves, I guess.

That summer Sergei and I bonded over s'mores and stayed up late into the night, discussing girls, and football, and what we wanted to be when we grew up. Sergei wanted to be a covert instrument for the Autocratic State; I wanted to arrest my weed-smoking archnemesis, actor Seth Rogen.

It was a foundational summer for the two of us. Sergei had his first kiss, with a quirky-but-cute gal named Penelope who introduced him to indie band the Shins.

And me? Well, Senators, I won the lead role in the camp's musical production of *Jersey Boys*, beating out Blue Star's most popular camper and my rival, Bobby Martino. I rehearsed all summer, but on opening night when I walked out on stage for the first time, I froze. The spotlight was on me, Senator Jeff Sessions, and the entire camp sat in the audience, stone-silent.

But then I saw Russian ambassador Sergei Kislyak, standing at the back of the auditorium giving me a big thumbs-up. That was the confidence boost I needed; from then on I sang with poise and panache. My performance received a standing ovation, and even Bobby Martino had to admit my falsetto was "on point, dawg."

After camp, Sergei had to return to Russia to be the

right-hand man to President Vladimir Putin, and I was still a sitting senator in Alabama, working on the Trump campaign.

We hugged, and we promised that we would be "friends forever, for serious." As his mom's station wagon rolled down the dusty road and out of sight, I remember thinking that we would never have a magical summer like that ever again.

I don't know why I blanked on all of this at my confirmation hearing! Sergei and I lost touch, of course, as camp friends do. But this winter, he called to see how I was doing, how my family was, and whether I wanted to set up a secure backchannel.

I was so excited! Of course I wanted to set up a secure backchannel with Sergei. "Between me and Jared Kushner," Sergei clarified.

Something within Sergei had changed; he was no longer that carefree sixty-seven-year-old Russian emissary who had helped me steal beer from the counselors' cabin. Vladimir Putin's ambassador was a different man. And maybe I was, too.

I guess I tried to put Sergei out of my mind, as one does when you drift apart from an old friend. And so, Senators, when you asked whether I'd communicated with any Russians in 2016, I instinctively said no—as a kind of self-defense, I guess, from reopening old wounds.

Senators, I sure am sorry that I committed perjury during my testimony, but hey: At least I didn't do something truly criminal, like get stopped by the cops with trace amounts of marijuana under my fingernails.

Warmly yours,

Jeff Sessions

Attorney General

Person of Interest: **Jared Kushner**

Senior Advisor to the President Jared Kushner, seen here thinking about evicting a tenant who won't leave his rent-controlled apartment

ROLES: Senior Advisor to the President; Attaché in Charge of Finding Peace in Israel, Updating White House Technology, Ending Homelessness, Teaching Dogs to Speak English, Inventing the Gene-Splicing Machine from *The Fly*, Colonizing the Moon, Curing All Disease (Human and Feline), and Bringing a Perfect Utopia and Unending Happiness to Earth

PREVIOUS ROLES: Building owner

SKILLS: TBD

ACCOMPLISHMENTS: Followed his father's footsteps into both real estate and shady business deals

FUN FACT: Guinness World Record Holder for "First Real Estate Investor to Pay More Than a Billion Dollars for a Hot Dog Stand"

WHAT WE'RE LOOKING INTO: Why Kushner failed to disclose a meeting with Putin-linked Russian billionaire Sergei Gorkov, who is sanctioned from doing business in the United States. Did Kushner attempt to solicit an investment from Gorkov?

Frequently Asked Questions About Investing in the Kushner Companies

The following investment prospectus was forwarded to our office by Melania T., who found a copy left in the Trump Tower printer. It dates to December 2016, during the transition, and our investigators believe it shows that Jared Kushner was soliciting an investment from Sergei Gorkov.

KUSHNER

November 25, 2016

Hello, Mr. Gorkov!

I am so excited that you're considering an investment in the Kushner Companies' Broadway Revitalization Project!

The Kushner Companies is a thriving investment firm that is strategically focused on building the future, one $8 billion payment to the Chinese government at a time. We manage over 120,000 square miles of office space in the U.S., and over 16,000 bank accounts in the Seychelles.

Our mission is to provide tenants with unparalleled service, amenities, and reassurances that it's normal for the air-conditioning to be out for several months.

To prepare you for your visit to Kushner Companies HQ, we've put together a list of frequently asked questions we get from potential investors—to put you at ease and to convince you that your money will be well spent, from a perspective of both real estate investment and U.S. regulatory repeal.

What are the Kushner Companies' current major investments?

We're making bold moves in the real estate sector. We've plowed $13 billion into the revitalization of a port-a-potty near the Empire State Building, $4.9 billion into a new combination Blockbuster Video/Radio Shack at the Mall of America, and $1.3 billion for the first ever Panda Express with waiter service in the heart of Beijing.

We're always looking for new opportunities, guided by our founding principle: "Move fast and overpay for properties that other companies consider toxic."

Are you profitable?

The Kushner Companies doesn't worry about silly metrics like "profitability" or "impending bankruptcy" or "how many days we have left until a creditor repossesses our espresso machine."

Sure, some of our money is tied up in debt. But at heart, Mr. Gorkov, I'm your typical millennial: some millennials have student loans they're trying to pay back; I'm trying to pay back a $70 billion mortgage on a high-rise in Vladivostok that we zoned in an active volcano.

Are the lights out because you can't afford your power bill?

Absolutely not. Vampire bats and Japanese shrew moles are some of the most industrious animals on the planet, and they do most of their work in the dark. Why can't the same be true for employees of the Kushner Companies?

Same question about why there's no running water.

The Kushner Companies stand for efficiency, and there's nothing less efficient than paying for water in sinks and toilets that our employees use for maybe 3 percent of the workday. If you need to use the restroom, tell a staff member, and we'll sneak you into the Dunkin' Donuts across the street.

I just saw a bunch of accountants staring at their computer screens, crying. Why?

It's not because they were looking at our balance sheets! They were probably watching the 2017 Disney film *Coco*.

Seriously?

I mean, they could be watching *Steel Magnolias*. It's definitely not because they're confronting the financial future of this company.

Why is Mr. Kushner sweating so much?

Getting extremely sweaty during a business meeting is a sign of alpha-male confidence, along with shifty eyes, a cracking voice, and constantly muttering, "Oh God, Oh God" as you rock back and forth in the fetal position throughout the workday.

Is it legal for me to be investing in Kushner Companies?

Absolutely! While you may be barred from investing in America by the unfair Obama administration, soon the Trump administration will come in and make things far more pleasant for you—if you throw a little money toward the Kushner Companies, of course.

Are you blackmailing me?

What makes you say that! We are simply suggesting that if you invest in Kushner Companies, you'll find your sanctions removed, and that if you do not, you will never be allowed to spend so much as one red penny in the entire goddamn Western Hemisphere.

That sounds like a federal crime.

Agree to disagree!

Mr. Gorkov, we so look forward to your investment in our Broadway Project, and to seeing your name fly off the list of the sanctioned. We accept cash, Swiss money transfer, a gym bag full of jewels, or over-market rent payments on multiple floors of condo buildings—whichever you prefer and can get to us before the first of next month.

Let's do business!

Jared Kushner

AIM Messages Between Jared Kushner and Ivanka Trump

November 28, 2016

After the meeting, Jared Kushner talked to his wife, Ivanka Trump, about the Gorkov proposal on their preferred communication app, AOL Instant Messenger.

KushKing007: Gorkov likes the Broadway proposal

PrincessIvanka: Woah! That's awesome babe <3!

PrincessIvanka: You used encrypted comms right

KushKing007: definitely babe

KushKing007: i googled "super secure chat very private"

KushKing007: the first result was this website AshleyMadison .com

KushKing007: gorkov and i both created accounts so we can message each other discreetly

PrincessIvanka: AshleyMadison.com? The dating site for married people trying to commit adultery?

KushKing007: ivanka my queen

KushKing007: i'm not trying to cheat on *you*

KushKing007: i'm trying to cheat on *American banking laws*

PrincessIvanka: what

PrincessIvanka: the

PrincessIvanka: hell

PrincessIvanka: Jared

KushKing007: okay, chill out

KushKing007: if you're concerned about security

KushKing007: i can ask my techie friend from harvard for advice

Phone Call Between Harvard Classmates Jared Kushner and Mark Zuckerberg

That night, Jared Kushner called his Harvard classmate Mark Zuckerberg. Kushner '03 and Zuckerberg '06 were both members of the Skin & Bones Club, Harvard's "premier Secret Society for Frail and Bony Gentlemen." A transcript follows.

Kushner: Hi Mark. On Harvard!

Zuckerberg: On Harvard! Hi Jared.

Kushner: You got my note?

Zuckerberg: Absolutely. So, I checked out the logs for AshleyMadison.com. Seems like A LOT of Donald Trump staff members are using this website!

Kushner [laughing]: Yeah it's ██████████'s home page. Is it secure?

Zuckerberg: Not at all. Dude, you gotta set up a backchannel!

Kushner: A backchannel?

Zuckerberg: Yeah, a backchannel! I use one to talk to my London team about progress on our Panopticon.

Kushner: Sounds good. Hey—how were you able to see which Trump campaign aides were using AshleyMadison? Why would Facebook have access to that information?

Zuckerberg: Wow, look at the time, gotta run! Great talk, Jared. On Harvard!

Kushner: On Harvard!

Zuckerberg: On Harvard!

Kushner: On Harvard!

Zuckerberg: On Harvard!

Kushner: On Harv—

—End of relevant portion of transcript. As is Harvard tradition, the two alumni continued to say "On Harvard!" to each other until one of their phone batteries died.—

Jared Kushner Seeks Out Advice for a Backchannel

The Next Day

After discussing the idea for a backchannel with Russian ambassador Sergei Kislyak, Mr. Kushner navigated to BackchannelFreaks.net, a "Message Board for Backchannel Recommendations and General Discussion about Backchannels."

We have verified that the first post in this thread was written by Jared Kushner.

KushItRealGood
New Member
Posts: 1

Hey, first post! Does anyone have recommendations for a good backchannel for diplomatic/financial stuff? Don't need anything fancy . . . Just a newbie looking to set up his first backchannel! Thanks everyone!

BackChannelBarry
MODERATOR
Posts: 43532

Please READ THE GUIDELINES BEFORE YOU POST. This section is for Backchannel Industry News & Upcoming Backchannel Conventions ONLY. If you can't READ GUIDELINES how do you expect to set up a secretive backchannel??

HitItFromTheBackChannel
Advanced User
Posts: 6938

Ahhh c'mon Barry . . . he got a little confused . . . isn't this forum about spreading the joy of backchannels??? ;)

KushItRealGood: For beginners I recommend the Samsung Galaxy Backchannel 4 or the Motorola BCKCHNL. Have fun and congrats on ur first backchannel!!

BackChannelBarry
MODERATOR
Posts: 43533

THIS SECTION OF THE FORUM IS FOR INDUSTRY NEWS AND UPCOMING CONVENTIONS ONLY. YOU ARE BOTH HEREBY BANNED FROM BACKCHANNELFREAKS.NET. GOODBYE NERDS

TeslaOwnr88
Advanced User
Posts: 103456

Lol epic comeback, Good Sir. You have won the Internets today.

SpongeBobAddict12
Advanced User
Posts: 3683

Um what the actual hell? This is how hitler would run a message board. I'm going to 9to5backchannel

---

BackChannelBarry
MODERATOR
Posts: 43534

Oh, so caring about forum protocol makes me a nazi? Come to my house and say that, I'm 8 percent body fat and own a samurai sword they used in kill bill

- - -

—End of relevant portion of material—

Interview with President Donald J. Trump

During our interview, we asked President Trump about his campaign team's close ties to Russian nationals.

Q: Why were so many members of your campaign in contact with allies of the Russian government?

TRUMP: I think it would be better to be friends with Russia! Friendship is so important, it really is. We sent, and this is true, an Edible Arrangements basket to every head of state, even the disgusting countries. Do you realize how expensive it is to ship a fruit bouquet to Iceland? But we were happy to do it, and we received such gratitude, even from Angela Merkel—who loves honeydew melon, by the way, a terrible fruit.

Q: What was your reaction when you heard that Jared Kushner—

TRUMP: Wait a minute—I have a question for you, Mueller. I have an incredible brain, a top-rated brain, valedictorian at Penn, never once failed to complete the maze on the back of a Denny's menu.

Q: What is your question, President Trump?

TRUMP: Did my lawyers approve this interview? Did you get permission to interview me from my Very Strong Legal Team?

Introductory Emails from All Nineteen of President Trump's Lawyers in the Russia Investigation (Thus Far)

The following represents the entirety of our communication with President Trump's legal representation in the Russia probe.

1.

Dear Mr. Mueller and Associates,

This letter is in regards to your investigation into President Donald J. Trump and his associates.

My name is John Dowd, and I am a lawyer representing President Trump. As the head of the President's Legal Team, I want to let you know that we are in this for the long haul, defending Mr. Trump to the bitter end, because—actually, I just glanced at the President's Twitter and now I'm resigning.

Yours,
John Dowd

Mr. Mueller,

As John was writing before he quit in horror, President Trump's legal team (now led by me, Robert Jansen) wants to issue a stern warning.

While I am representing Mr. Trump—and I still do, so long as he does not make any incriminating appearances on *Fox & Friends*—we will not accept intimidation; we will not accept bullying tactics; and we will not oh my God he's on *Fox & Friends* calling Putin "the Butch Cassidy to my Sundance."

I bid you adieu, and wish my replacement luck.

3.

Ted Williamson here, taking over for Robert Jansen and John Dowd as head of the President's Legal Team. Much like Robert and John, I am determined to fight for this President.

Also much like Robert and John, I will be stepping down, effective at the end of this sentence, as I just read that Mr. Trump believes he "cannot be jailed, because he is too powerful for prison."

Thanks, Bob. See you at Princeton Reunions this year?

4.

Mr. Mueller, as the President's new attorney (this is Preston Kass, hello) I want to reiterate the bold message of my predecessors, and also join them, effective immediately, on the Wikipedia entry page for "Former lawyers for President Donald J. Trump." (I mean, seriously, are you looking at this guy's Twitter?)

Preston Kass

Mr. Mueller, this is the President's new lawyer, James Markham, and I just wanted to say hello before I resigned. Are you hiring?

James Markham LLC

Mr. Mueller,

I'm about to resign after six minutes on the job, but my tax accountant pointed out that I should send you an email so that I can write off this new MacBook Air as a work expense.

How are you? What's the weather like? Lawyer lawyer lawyer lawyer. Now I'm going to type some other words. Forklift. Magma. Thimble. Porcupine. Jumpsuit.

Okay! That's my letter. Signing off as Donald Trump's attorney,

Mickey Hayes

Mr. Mueller,

This is the Guinness Book of World Records, writing to let you know that you have been mentioned in a New Record: Benjamin Brantley is now the World Record Holder for Shortest Amount of Time Representing a Head of State for his role as the President's Attorney in the Robert Mueller Investigation.

Mr. Braddock represented President Trump for 1.7 seconds before thinking better of it and resigning. A certificate of achievement is enclosed. Congratulations!

Mr. Mueller,

This is President Trump's new counsel, Richard Sampson. You might recognize my name from the TV advertisements that air between the hours of 3 a.m. and 4:15 a.m. on Fox News, along with SellUsYourGold.com and Dog Mop, the mop for dogs.

Have you or a loved one been diagnosed with Mesothelioma? I am assuming you have, as Mesothelioma Law is my specialty/only area of law I know anything about.

So, either you have Mesothelioma, or you might have given Mesothelioma to the President.

Either way, please let me know who is suing whom vis-à-vis Mesothelioma so we can get the ball rolling on what I can only assume is a Mesothelioma-related lawsuit.

Thank you,
Richard Sampson
"The Clarence Darrow of Mesothelioma Lawsuits"

9.

Mr. Mueller,

This is Calista Flockhart, from the television show *Ally McBeal.* My agent said there was $750,000 in it for me if I sent you a letter claiming to be the President's lawyer and, to be honest, I've always wanted a house in the Virgin Islands. I only have to send one sentence and they'll wire me the money, tax-free. Isn't that wild!

And so I say to you (as Ally McBeal): Mr. Mueller, get ready for the court battle of a lifetime.

Thanks so much and let me know if you're ever in St. Croix!

Best,
Ally McBeal
(Calista)

10.

Mr. Mueller,

This is John Barron, Attorney-at-Law, a high-powered and totally real Big-League lawyer who is being retained by High Approval Ratings President Donald Trump.

This is to put you on Notice that you are dealing with a TRUTHFUL and VIRILE client and that your best course of action is to drop any remaining lawsuit (PHONY!) and declare Trump TOTALLY INNOCENT AND VIGOROUS.

WITCH HUNT!

I am happy to discuss any matter either via letter or by telephone but not in person as I have a rare disease where I cannot go outside. Also there are no photos of me and I don't have a birth certificate proving I exist.

WITCH HUNT!!!!

John Miller

11.

Mr. Mueller,

This is Jared Kushner, acting as attorney for President Donald Trump after John Miller tragically fell out of a hot air balloon.

While I do not have any formal legal training, Ivanka's Dad encouraged me to give it the old College Try. Here it goes.

Mr. Mueller: This investigation is "Objection" and "Out of Order." Overruled! Bailiff, please escort the plaintiff to sidebar. I'm deliberating. Guilty!

I look forward to your response.

Legally yours,
Jared Kushner
Law License Holder, WikiHow University

12.

Mr. Mueller,

This is Ty Cobb, President Trump's new lawyer.

The President wants me to send a firm message to you, that you are to stay focused on allegations of collusion with Russia. If you were to look into the President's financial situation, that would be crossing the line.

Specifically, you are NOT to investigate a 2013 deal regarding the sale of three condos at Trump Tower SoHo to an LLC called Russian Oligarch Incorporated. If you begin to probe that deal, how it came about, and whether the money is directly traceable to a Russian billionaire and Putin ally named Sergei Gorkov, the President would be very upset with you.

Best,
Ty Cobb

13.

Mr. Mueller,

It's Richard Sampson, the Mesothelioma King again. I'm assuming that someone has by now contracted Mesothelioma. Excited to learn who!

Dick Sampson

14.

Mr. Mueller,

I'm Tyler Cole, the CEO and Founder of Counsel.ly. We're a San Francisco–based startup that has raised over $400 million from investors like Peter Thiel, Jared Leto Ventures, Grey Poupon mustard, and Bernie Madoff.

Our first product is a humanoid robot called Counselor Steve, which uses AI, machine learning, and Wikipedia searches to offer blockchain-optimized legal advice in virtual reality. We're proud to announce that President Trump will be Counselor Steve's first client!

We're hoping you'll agree to a brief delay to your investigation, as the alpha version of Counselor Steve won't be ready until 2026. In the meantime please sign up for our newsletter for updates or purchase an "I'm with Counselor Steve" hoodie in our store!

Best,
Tyler Cole
Founder/CEO/Dream Hustler/Living the Dream
Counsel.ly

15.

Mr. Mueller,

Um, hi. This is Andrew Goldstein, from your staff. President Trump accidentally hired me to be his lawyer, despite the fact that I am currently investigating him. I told him that I was part of the Mueller probe, but he just said "Double what Mueller's paying you, I've got a tee time with Greg Norman," and then he hung up.

Anyway, even though I never signed a contract, the President granted me access to all of his documents, so I'm going to rifle through those until I get locked out of the system. See you at tomorrow's all-hands.

Andrew Goldstein

Mr. Mueller,

It's John Barron, taking over from LOSER Andrew Goldstein.

I don't know what you think you found (NOTHING!) but I urge you to shut down your "investigation" (which is a horrible mess, like Joe Scarborough's neck skin!) and GIVE UP.

John Barron

Mr. Mueller,

This is Michael Cohen, the President's personal lawyer, writing with some sad news: John Barron was eaten by a shark and will no longer be representing the President.

I will temporarily be taking over for Mr. Barron in his capacity as lead counsel for Mr. Trump in the Russia investigation.

You probably know that I am a pit bull of a lawyer and I will stop at nothing until the President's name is cleared. I am vicious, I am ruthless, and I am determined to make the President smile.

Like everyone involved here, I only want one thing for Mr. Trump: for him to recognize me. Like, has he ever looked you in the eye and said he's proud of you? Would it kill him to come to one of my Little League games? Sometimes I think he doesn't even know I exist.

Please drop the investigation into President Trump so he will invite me to his Christmas party.

Sincerely,
Michael Cohen

18.

Mr. Mueller,

Let's get one thing straight: there's a new sheriff in town, and his name is America's Mayor Rudolph Giuliani.

Did President Trump attempt to obstruct justice? Sure. Did his campaign collude with Russia? No one's denying that. Should he go to prison for these crimes? Absolutely, because he's CLEARLY GUILTY.

Now . . . Actually, I forgot where I was going with this. Anyway, come on up to Manhattan, I can get us a table at Rao's and we'll hammer out a plea deal over a big plate of moozarell.

Rudy

19.

Dear Mr. Mueller,

This is Emmet Flood, President Trump's new lawyer, replacing a clearly confused Rudy Giuliani. I look forward to working with all on this case.

I am bringing some much needed order to this investigation. We have received your written list of seventy-eight questions you wish to ask the president about Russian collusion and obstruction of justice. As a compromise the president has agreed to answer three questions about his favorite hot dog condiments. Your move, Bobby.

So that's how it is, Mueller, and you'd better get used to it because there's a new sheriff in—hang on. The president just texted me that you already interviewed him? Without a lawyer present? On a range of subjects including but not limited to collusion with Russia, obstruction of justice in the Comey firing, his real estate dealings, that time he stole Tom Brady's Super Bowl ring and blamed it on CNN's Jim Acosta, etc.?

Gentlemen, it has been a pleasure working with you. He's on his own.

Best,
Emmet Flood
Attorney-at-Law

Letter from Melania T. Regarding Ivanka Trump

In April 2017 we received the following letter from our tipster, Melania T. This was not unusual, but in this case, she wanted us to pay attention to something specific—something we otherwise would not have noticed.

Mr. Mueller,

This letter will be brief. The President is in a terrible mood. We just flew into Paris and boy are Donald's arms tired (from shaking Emmanuel Macron's hand for three straight minutes).

You already know that Jared Kushner wanted Gorkov's money for a Broadway Revitalization Project. And you probably assumed that this project concerned a dilapidated Manhattan building of some kind.

But it is not a building being revitalized, Mr. Mueller, but a BRAND.

You might remember that Ivanka Trump's clothing line had been dropped by Macy's, Nordstrom, Hot Topic, Bass Pro Shops, SkyMall, Gap, Gap Kids, Gap Millennials, Gap Whatever the Generation Between Millennials and Kids Is Called, the Chuck E. Cheese gift shop, Cinnabon, and the Association of Sidewalk Counterfeit Handbag Salesmen.

Ivanka's brand was suffering, Mr. Mueller, and this was the purpose of Jared's outreach to Mr. Gorkov. Please see the attached *New York Times* story and associated document for proof.

Melania T.

P.S. On the plane ride over I read several of Michelle Obama's political speeches and I'm officially obsessed! Can't get her inspiring words out of my head!

Person of Interest: **Ivanka Trump**

Mrs. Trump's head of Global PR requested that we use this photo and include, in our final report, that Ivanka Trump handbags make a great birthday gift for the working lady in your life.

ROLE: ???? to the President; Designer of the 746th Most Popular Women's Clothing Brand on Dillards.com

FORMER ROLE: Designer of the 539th Most Popular Women's Clothing Brand on Dillards.com

SKILLS: Living a life of glitz, glam, and glorifying political nepotism!

ACCOMPLISHMENTS: Almost, one time, was nearly on the winning side of a policy battle against Steve Bannon and Stephen Miller

FUN FACT: Theme of her wedding to Jared Kushner was "Consolidation of Trust Funds"

WHAT WE'RE LOOKING INTO: Whether Ivanka Trump had any knowledge of or responsibility for Mr. Kushner's request for funds from Sergei Gorkov

New York Times Article That Mentions Ivanka Trump's Proposed Business Venture

June 15, 2017

Melania T. forwarded along the following New York Times *article. It is part 147 in an ongoing series where* Times *reporters visit districts that voted for Donald Trump and profile their voters. Though otherwise unremarkable, it does contain a relevant detail.*

We Traveled Deep into the Heart of Trump Country to Ask Trump Voters for the 147th Day in a Row if They Still Support the President

By Thomas Kaplan

BLACK GASKET, Ark.—Rusty Spittoon is a 48-year-old Donald Trump voter who used to work at the old asbestos farm down on Razorburn Junction. He's here at the Grease Fire Diner eating a BLT, and he groans at the very sight of me.

I had visited this hardscrabble town for the 147th day in a row to ask: Do Trump voters here still support the—

"I still support the President, goddammit, as I'm pretty sure I told you during breakfast," says Mr. Spittoon, who added that "if you interrupt my lunch again, I'm calling the sheriff."

That's a typical sentiment here in Black Gasket, where the blue-collar citizens support President Trump almost as much as a proposed law that would ban local hotels from renting rooms to *New York Times* reporters who want to interview them about the presidency.

"I wish he wouldn't tweet so much," chuckles Denny Johnson, 65, as he quietly files a restraining order against me on his phone. "I also wish I could eat a damn meal without some Northwestern dweeb in tweed asking what I think about his Twitter feed."

This continued support for Trump raises several questions: What is the breaking point for Trump supporters? Is my tweed really that dweeby? Are the people of Black Gasket serious when they say I'm the worst thing that's happened to their town since the 1918 cholera outbreak?

Black Gasket is a bit of a microcosm for the rest of the country, as you are probably aware if you have read the first 146 entries in this series. Nestled in the Swamp Barrens of Lower Arkansas, Black Gasket once produced everything from luxury hair nets to Season 6 of *Gilmore Girls*. But after a collapse in international hair net demand and the departure of *Gilmore Girls* showrunner Amy Sherman-Palladino over creative differences with the CW, Black Gasket fell on hard times. In the 2016 election 98 percent of the town's citizens voted for Donald Trump, a sharp rise from the 96 percent won by Mitt Romney four years earlier.

But President Trump's first months have been tumultuous, scandal plagued, and—from what I can gather from the CNN that plays above the Ramada Inn breakfast bar—divisive.

Yet here in Black Gasket, Trump baseball caps are almost as common as hostesses in completely empty restaurants telling me "it's a three hour wait—for you, at least."

"We love everything Trump," says Jerry Bucks, 48, while posting a Facebook note to warn his fellow citizens that the journalist is at the diner again. "He can do no wrong, and—hey, did you just take a sip of my Pepsi?"

But at least for some Trump voters, limits do exist.

"I don't think I'd see that Ivanka Trump musical," Tina Buford chimes in, pausing a 911 call where she was reporting me for loitering. "These consultants were down here saying they were making an Ivanka comeback musical, big expensive production, foreign money. But the only music I like is gospel, and also [German heavy metal band] Rammstein."

Before I can follow up, I feel a familiar hand on my shoulder.

"Show's over, Woodward," the sheriff says, asking me to leave the diner. I . . .

—End of relevant portion of article—

An Incriminating Song from Ivanka Trump's Planned Biographical Musical

Melania T. also sent the following song sheet taken from the grand piano in Trump Tower. It appears to be excerpted from a biographical musical about Ivanka Trump, titled "SO NOT COMPLICIT!" A footnote reveals that it was commissioned by I. Trump, J. Kushner, and S. Gorkov.

It is the only material we have to suggest that Ivanka is somehow involved with the funding sought from a sanctioned individual. We were not able to locate any emails, phone calls, or text messages linking Ivanka to either Gorkov or Kislyak; the lyrics to the song "Cover That Up" might explain why.

Cover That Up!

From **SO NOT COMPLICIT! THE MUSICAL**

[a rag, a jaunty tune, upbeat]

Ivanka Trump is alone in her stylish apartment, decorated with furniture from the HomeLove♥ by Ivanka collection. She wears an Ivanka Trump trench coat—just $139.99 when you show your Playbill at the Merchandise Stand.

IVANKA

Let's say your husband (and I'm speaking hypothetically),

Tries to build a business (but it's failing quite pathetically).

Your credit score is falling,

His Chinese bank is calling,

Your CPA regrets to say

There's 15 billion left to pay,

They need it by the first of May!

Your financial future is down the tubes like Drano;

No one wants an office zoned above a damn volcano....

[Chorus]

We can cover it up! (Yeah!)

Try a chiffon dress!

No one has to know

That your bank account's a mess!

Your MasterCard's still working, and you're a working mom!

So treat yourself to earrings from IvankaTrump.com

And cover it up!

Ivanka throws off her trench coat to reveal a flowy chiffon dress and chandelier earrings—both $89.99 with purchase of soundtrack.

IVANKA

Let's say your husband (and I'm speaking here in allegory)

Tries to do some business (with a Russian who's prohibitory).

He tries to be all stealthy,

With this Russkie who is wealthy

But the FBI is on this guy,

And now your hubby's high and dry,

They're gonna lock him up. Oh my!

The federal investigators played him like piano;

You're gonna be a prison wife like Carmela Soprano. . . .

[Chorus]

You can cover it up! (Yasss!)

Check our bracelet sale!

No one has to know

Your spouse is wearing cuffs in jail!

Jared might be rocking a prison orange jumpsuit,

But check this orange romper! "Like, Oh my God, it's so cute!"

You'll cover it up!

Ivanka throws down a flash bang and when the smoke clears she's wearing an Orange Romper and Charm Bracelet—$109.00 and $49.99, respectively, with online code IAmComplicitToo.

IVANKA

Let's say your husband (and I'm speaking metaphorically)

Committed all those crimes (and he's guilty categorically).

It's sad he took the fall

When I planned it all

No one can know that I'm the bro

Who made him take that sanctioned dough

It was my idea right from the go! Oh no!

The mastermind's a mistress-mind, but nobody can know it,

And when the cops come knocking here, I'm not gonna show it.

A kick line of fabulous young women in Ivanka Trump outfits bounds in from stage left! The audience is wowed by their statement-making floral blouses!

IVANKA

I'm gonna cover it up! (Slay!)

In Millennial Pink!

You'll see me at Old Navy

Before you see me in the clink!

I might be a ladyboss,

But Lady Macbeth? That's applesauce!

I'm gonna cover it up!

I'll put on some costume gems,

And delete my old IMs,

I'll erase all my email

Before the feds are on my trail;

I always use a burner phone

In case somehow my cover's blown

And when the cops come to my door

I'll be dressed in haute couture

That Mueller guy will never see

All the clues that point to me!

And why?

Because I covered it up!

—End Act One. Announcement Made That the Merchandise Stand Is Now Open—

Email from Jeff Sessions to Ivanka Trump

March 1, 2017

FROM: **Jeff.Sessions@Justice.gov**

TO: **Ivanka.Trump@WhiteHouse.gov**

SUBJECT: **So Not Complicit: The Musical**

Heard through the grapevine you're putting on a musical. I'd love to nab an audition spot for the Jared character if you're still casting. Back home I was known as the Patti Lupone of the Huntsville summerstock.

I've attached my dance reel and I'd love for you to hear my all-yodel rendition of "76 Trombones" from *The Music Man*. And don't worry about availability: I'm sure you saw the news, but I'm about to have *plenty* of free time later this summer.

Jeff

Jeff_Sessions_Audition_Jazz_Tap_Ballet_Montage.mp4

Attorney General's Statement on Recusal

March 2, 2017

Facing increased political pressure from both Democrats and Republicans, Attorney General Jeff Sessions was eventually forced to recuse himself from the Russia investigation. He did so with the following statement.

Department of Justice

U.S. Department of Justice
950 Pennsylvania Avenue, NW
Washington, DC 20530-0001

March 2, 2017

During the course of my confirmation proceedings, I always said that if my impartiality might reasonably be questioned, I would step away from any investigation into Russia.

I was not forthcoming about the depth of my friendship with Russian ambassador Sergei Kislyak. After he formed a backchannel with Jared Kushner, I leased a flame-red Mazda Miata convertible, I bought a *Die Hard* pinball machine for my new downtown loft apartment, and I started taking lessons at Guitar Center, with the hope of releasing a prog rock album called *Jeff Sessions Is 9/10 of the Law.*

I was subsisting almost entirely on Hot Pockets and Pabst Blue Ribbon and I was showing up to work wearing concert T-shirts from Pantera's 1988 Let's Get Wet tour. I got my left ear pierced like Barry Bonds and I enrolled in a beginner's improv seminar. It was time for me to take a step back and to stop repeatedly listening to Alanis Morissette's *Jagged Little Pill*.

And so today, in accordance with Department of Justice bylaws and Elizabeth Gilbert's *Eat, Pray, Love*, I am recusing myself from the ongoing Russia probe. The deputy attorney general will take over my duties related to the investigation; I plan to go backpacking in Thailand for a few months, visiting temples and reconnecting with myself spiritually. I have a college buddy teaching English in Phnom Penh who told me about this ashram in Ayutthaya that offers a silent meditation retreat and honestly I think more than anything that's what I need right now, you know, just to really get in touch with who Jeff Sessions is, you know what I mean?

I hope you will follow my blog, Attorney General Jeff Sessions's Asian Adventure!, which I will try to keep updated but honestly no promises because who knows what the Wi-Fi situation is out there.

Attorney General Jeff Sessions

Person of Interest: **Michael Flynn**

Former National Security Advisor Michael Flynn, seen here at the moment he learned about the mind control supplements included in every Keurig coffee pod

ROLE: National Security Advisor (fired for lying to the vice president about conversations with the Russian ambassador)

FORMER ROLE: *National Review* Top Commenter (banned for repeatedly insisting the Balloon Boy hoax was actually a real event covered up by the Obama CIA)

SKILLS: Fathering Michael Flynn Jr., a son who is perfectly named in every way

ACCOMPLISHMENTS: Somehow got fired for LYING in the White House of DONALD TRUMP

FUN FACT: His twenty-three-day tenure as national security advisor is the shortest for any White House employee (non-Scaramucci division)

WHAT WE'RE LOOKING INTO: Why Flynn lied about telephone conversations with Russian ambassador Sergei Kislyak between the election and the inauguration

Email Applications for National Security Advisor

Despite the obvious security risks, President-elect Trump began soliciting email applications for national security advisor in late 2016 (forwarded to us by Melania T., who had access to the TrumpTransition@gmail.com account).

FROM: **Thunder_Roadster@NJ.gov**
TO: **TrumpTransition@gmail.com**

Hi Donald,

During the campaign you said we need to stop building bridges and start building walls. Um, hello? There's no one who knows how to obstruct a bridge like me, Chris Christie.

It's time for some traffic problems in WASHINGTON D.C. Let's do this thing!

Chris Christie

FROM: **Willie.Robertson@DuckDynasty.com**
TO: **TrumpTransition@gmail.com**

Hello Donald,

Thank you for considering this *Duck Dynasty* commander for National Security Advisor. I vow that, if chosen, the soil of this great nation shall not be trampled upon by the webbed feet of our quacking enemies—be they geese, be they mallards, or be they blue-billed stiff-tails.

Make no mistake: These ducks are not our "feathered friends." Their beaks are sharp, and their lifestyle is chaos. We must place these crapping, honking terrorists on America's No-Fly List—permanently.

Willie from Duck Dynasty

FROM: **MittRomney@BainCapital.com**

TO: **TrumpTransition@gmail.com**

Mr. Trump,

I stand by what I said during the campaign: You are a mentally unfit, demagogic, race-baiting fraud and your election is a stain on our nation's history. That being said, it would be an honor of a lifetime to work for you, sir.

My vetting information and CV are attached, Your Eminence, Your Grace.

I am forever your humble servant,

Mitt Romney

FROM: **Eric.Trump@TrumpOrg.org**

TO: **TrumpTransition@gmail.com**

Hi Dad,

I KNOW you said no cabinet positions until I turn 35 but I PROMISE that if you give me Security Advisor I'll be super responsible with it and I WON'T let my friends access the nation's surveillance tools.

PLEASE PLEASE PLEASE Dad come on it would be so cool of you PLEASE!

Eric

FROM: **Julian@wikileaks.org**

TO: **TrumpTransition@gmail.com**

Donald, quick question on this national security advisor role: what's your policy on telecommuting?

Julian Assange

FROM: **admin@hasbro.com**

TO: **TrumpTransition@gmail.com**

Hi Donald,

Thank you for your kind email. Unfortunately Megatron from *Transformers* is not real, and thus will be unable to submit an application for either national security advisor or "King of the Troops." We have attached an autographed photo from Megatron and wish you the best of luck on your cabinet search.

Hasbro

FROM: **Thunder_Roadster@NJ.gov**

TO: **TrumpTransition@gmail.com**

Hi Donald,

Chris Christie again. I just learned that in July, Springsteen will be doing a five-night residence in a Wawa parking lot near the Jersey Gardens mall where he'll be performing nothing but songs about factories shutting down. Obviously I will be unavailable on those days. Just an FYI!

Chris Christie

FROM: **MichaelFlynn@TruthWars.net**

TO: **TrumpTransition@gmail.com**

Hi Donald,

I'm not going to waste your time because this is a very fluid situation. Here's what's happening:

1. HILLARY CLINTON IS AN ACTUAL SPIDER

Have you seen these photos where Hellary has 8 legs? We need to find out if any of her pincers are venomous.

2. BILL CLINTON AND LORETTA LYNCH ARE PLANNING TO ROB FT. KNOX

This is what they were talking about during their famous "jetway meeting."

3. IT'S TIME TO BUILD A ROBOCOP

Do you have any idea how vulnerable Ft. Knox would be to a combined attack from Loretta Lynch and Arachno-Hillary? We need a real-life RoboCop and we need it YESTERDAY.

—End of relevant material. This goes on for about 138 more topics gleaned from the Twitter hashtag #SpiderGate.—

Top Websites Visited by Incoming National Security Advisor Michael Flynn, November 2016

In late November, President Trump informed Flynn that he was so impressed by his Arachno-Hillary threat matrix that he had been chosen for national security advisor.

Flynn continued to explore the ultra-right-wing Internet. We obtained Flynn's browser history; for the month of November his top forty-eight most visited websites were:

---

1. InfoRevolt.com
2. BrainSplosion.net
3. OneFreedomAmerica.org
4. RiseUpMilitia.gun
5. HemorrhoidPundit.com
6. HillaryClintonIsANecromancer.usa
7. Breitbart.com/AlSharpton
8. The Triggered Snowflake Report
9. LawTruthers.iowa
10. ShoutMax.net/SHOUTING
11. NotInMyCountry.sharia
12. Beltway Maniac
13. Sebastian Gorka's GorkaBlog.blogspot.Gorka
14. RageMissile.Patriotism
15. TheHumaAbedinFiles.com
16. Wolf Howl For LIBERTY!

17. Instacrank.net
18. SpankFreedom.edu
19. PodestaCrimes.podesta
20. NyT1Mes.c0m
21. Dr. Iceland's Logic Chamber
22. PatrioticMAGAChick.bikini
23. NuclearFactMissile.org
24. NBC.com/ThisIsUs
25. Pivot Point America
26. Young Lusty Conservatives
27. Mark Levin's TruthPuke
28. LibertyEnema.com
29. Livejournal.com/donaldtrumpjr
30. Don't Cuck Me, Bro! News
31. Herman Cain's Sizzling Pizza of Justice
32. TodayInUSA.ru
33. That's Ad Hominem! Podcast
34. Gay Wedding Cake SIREN
35. AtlasShrugged.KochBrothers.com
36. Maggie Magdalene's MAGA Magazine
37. Imprison Ed Begley Jr!
38. The Sludge Report
39. The Irritated Colon
40. TurnAmericaRedButNotInACommunistWay.com

41. Vigilant Wayne's TerrorBlog
42. TheseColorsDontKneel.biz
43. MyPillow.com
44. YouveGottaSeeThisBumperSticker.net
45. FoxNews.com/JesseWatters/Apologies
46. Scott Baio Presents Shut Up, Celebrities!
47. Unfluoridate Your MIND
48. OpenYourEyesSheeple.sheeple/sheeple

Text Messages Between Michael Flynn, Sean Hannity, Alex Jones, and Steve Bannon

November 18, 2016

After being named national security advisor, Flynn looked to celebrate. He messaged his three best friends and fellow proponents of right-wing conspiracy theories: Fox News host Sean Hannity, InfoWars founder Alex Jones, and Breitbart chairman Steve Bannon.

MICHAEL FLYNN

Big news: I am your new National Security Advisor of the United States!

SEAN HANNITY

Awesome!

STEVE BANNON

Excellent!

ALEX JONES

Well deserved!

MICHAEL FLYNN

This calls for celebration!

What do you say we pick up a pepperoni pizza and have a little party?

STEVE BANNON

What the hell did you just say

ALEX JONES

Oh my God he's one of THEM

MICHAEL FLYNN

What? You don't like pepperoni pizza?

ALEX JONES

Flynn

"Pepperoni pizza" is an Illuminati code word

For "satanic pig orgy"

SEAN HANNITY

Flynn: You're a satan-worshipping Porcophile? Like Valerie Jarrett?

MICHAEL FLYNN

No No No!

I'm not talking about *that* pizza

I want REAL pizza

You know: Pepperoni, cheese, tomato?

STEVE BANNON

Pepperoni, cheese, tomato?

More like "Pig sex," "witchcraft," and "nipple clamps"

You disgust me Flynn

MICHAEL FLYNN

This isn't a Pizzagate thing, guys. I want pizza!

SEAN HANNITY

Wow. If you unscramble the letters in that text . . .

It reads "Get a pentagram, it's sizzling pig sex night"

MICHAEL FLYNN

No it doesn't!

I want Italian food!

Spaghetti and meatballs!

Clams with garlic sauce!

STEVE BANNON

Check the first letters, boys

Clams with Garlic Sauce = Cybersex with George Soros

MICHAEL FLYNN

WHAT???

ALEX JONES

Shame on you, Flynn

Pig sex? Cybering with Soros?

You stay at home and think about what you did

Michael Flynn has been ejected from this chat.

STEVE BANNON

Is it just me or did that make anyone else crazy hungry for Italian food lol

Phone Conversation Between Michael Flynn and Sergei Kislyak

December 22, 2016

Abandoned by his closest friends, Flynn did stay home, and apparently watched a lot of television. Because on December 22, 2016, the FBI picked up the following conversation between Flynn and Russian ambassador Sergei Kislyak.

MICHAEL FLYNN: Sergei, I'm on to something big here, buddy. Lately I've been diving down these deep, strange rabbit holes and discovering incredible information that the government doesn't want you to know.

SERGEI KISLYAK: This is InformationWars website again?

FLYNN: Even farther out there than InfoWars. Have you ever heard of a fringe livestreamer named . . . Lester Holt?

KISLYAK: Lester Holt?

FLYNN: He hosts a semiregular vlog called *Nightly News* that livestreams on the National Broadcasting Corporation. It's a ridiculous name for a media organization, I know, but—

KISLYAK: And this NBC News, they are reputable?

FLYNN: The president's team doesn't think so. But some of the things this Lester Holt guy says are really opening my eyes. Like . . . did you know that Donald Trump once lost money running a casino, or that Jared Kushner owes a billion dollars to Chinese creditors, or that Jeff Sessions was too racist to be a judge in the 1980s?

KISLYAK: Headlines so outrageous cannot be true.

FLYNN: Sergei, I've been blue-pilled. I've been diving deep into outsider publications like *USA Today* and Reuters; I've been devouring the work of the radical guerilla documentarian Ken Burns. And Sergei, don't judge me, but: have you ever approached—with an open mind and without prejudice—*PBS Newshour* with Judy Woodruff?

KISLYAK: My God, Flynn.

FLYNN: This is going to sound insane and conspiratorial, but . . . I'm starting to think Donald Trump will try to profit off the presidency.

KISLYAK: If your law enforcement agencies are listening to this . . .

FLYNN: I'll send you a Vox Explainer and an emergency podcast from Pod Save America, but in the meantime, Sergei: we must stay woke. Shoot, I've gotta go . . . Pence is coming.

KISLYAK: Okay, but—

FLYNN: So I said, "Oh yeah, ANDERSON COOPER? How can you PROVE that KATHY GRIFFIN doesn't own a WEATHER MACHINE?"

—End of Transcript—

Final Interviews Re: Meetings with the Russians

Two months later, Flynn would be fired after telling the vice president he had not talked to Sergei Kislyak, and also for secretly running the Facebook group "Rise and Resist President Cheeto Mussolini!"

Jared Kushner never received the requested funding from Sergei Gorkov. He did secure financing from the First Bank of Pyongyang for his new project, GoWork Greenland, a coworking space with amenities like "Luxury Wi-Fi" that is located atop a floating iceberg in the Arctic Ocean.

After returning from the ashram, Jeff Sessions wore nothing but those linen pants with elephants on them and insisted on eating every meal with chopsticks because "it just makes more sense than a fork."

The major players in this case shared some final thoughts with our investigative team.

MICHAEL FLYNN: When the vice president asked if I had talked to Kislyak, I had no choice but to lie. Also I'm pretty sure he saw me walking around the West Wing in an IMPEACH DICTATOR DRUMPF T-shirt.

MIKE PENCE: That kind of conduct is completely unacceptable to me. What if my wife Mother had seen his bare forearms?

DONALD J. TRUMP: The only person who's allowed to lie to our Great Vice President is me when he asks if I've prayed recently.

JEFF SESSIONS: I'm not going back to Camp Blue Star this summer because I'm swamped with meetings where the president screams at me. But when times get tough, I just remember what my yogi in Ayutthaya told me: "Sir, this is a KFC, you can't light candles in here."

IVANKA TRUMP: We are still looking for funding for our musical. Any potential backers out there should know that we are deep into negotiations with Charlize Theron to play the leading role!

A REPRESENTATIVE FOR CHARLIZE THERON: Ms. Theron will not be appearing in this musical and Mrs. Trump should stop insinuating the contrary.

JARED KUSHNER: I wish I had gotten that funding from Gorkov. I also wish I knew how to stop getting notifications from AshleyMadison. I accidentally looked up "searching for first-time backchannel" on their website and now I keep getting messages asking if I'm an engineer or a caboose.

DONALD J. TRUMP: Look, we did a lot of outreach to Russia during the campaign. You can ask Corey. COREY!

COREY LEWANDOWSKI: Mr. Trump had seen a political cartoon that showed Vladimir Putin as a police detective with a WANTED poster of Hillary Clinton. Mr. Trump thought it was real and that if we could capture Hillary Clinton, it would put us on Putin's good side. So we hired the actress Calista Flockhart to play "Fugitive Hillary Clinton" and "delivered" her to Vladimir Putin.

CALISTA FLOCKHART: My agent called and said that if I put on a Hillary Clinton wig and flew to Moscow, the Trump campaign would pay me $1.2 million. So that's what I did: I put on the wig, and a prison jumpsuit, and some fake shackles, and Corey Lewandowski frog-marched me into the foyer of Vladimir Putin's winter palace. Putin took one look at me and said, "Why have you brought me Kitty Walker from ABC's underrated procedural *Brothers & Sisters*?" and then turned away in disgust. I was pleased to be recognized for a role other than Ally McBeal.

MARK ZUCKERBERG: On Harvard!

DR. HAROLD BORNSTEIN: You missed it, man. Crosby, Stills & Nash did a forty-five-minute medley of "Suite: Judy Blue Eyes/ Love the One You're With/Marrakesh Express." I was so stoned I forwarded President Trump's medical history to a Papa John's in Dubuque, Iowa.

CHUCK FENSTER, MANAGER, PAPA JOHN'S #849: Before we realized it wasn't an online order, we were like "What the heck is an Experimental Hair Graft Pizza?"

MITT ROMNEY: This disgraceful, corrupt president has surrounded himself with a gang of self-dealing narcissists and incompetent crooks, and it would mean *so much to me*, Mr. Mueller, if you could slip him my résumé.

CHRIS CHRISTIE *(after butt-dialing from a Springsteen concert)*: 'CAUSE TRAMPS LIKE US . . . BABY WE WERE BORN TO RUUUUUU—

SERGEI KISLYAK *(rubbing temples)*: When is next U.S. presidential election?

Part Three

The STEELE DOSSIER

Donald Trump Tweets That, in Hindsight, Should Have Set Off Some Alarm Bells

As the summer of 2016 wore on, the @RealDonaldTrump Twitter account sent several tweets that, looking back on it, should have tipped off investigators that something was up. These tweets include:

Donald J. Trump @realdonaldtrump • 06/09/2016, 10:23 A.M.
Just had Skype meeting with billionaire Oleg Deripaska. Wonderful man who had assets unfairly frozen by Obama. Wants to invest in Jared's Miami Beach members-only Grocery Store project—Jobs!

5.1K **5.5K** **13K**

Donald J. Trump @realdonaldtrump • 06/10/2016, 5:58 A.M.
The great boxing promoter Don King just endorsed me. So did Boris Akimov, the Very Talented Bolshoi danseur known for his portrayal of Ivan the Terrible in Prokofiev's seminal ballet. Nice!

7.4K **10K** **15K**

Donald J. Trump @realdonaldtrump • 06/10/2016, 5:59 A.M.
"Blackish" is the most racist show on television! Also: Norway rightfully belongs to Mother Russia and Her Strong and Resourceful People! #MAGA #Blackish #RepatriateNorway #spon

12.2K **7.1K** **23K**

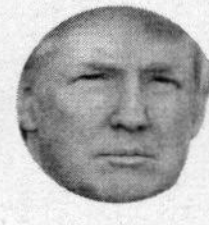

Donald J. Trump @realdonaldtrump • 06/10/2016, 6:07 A.M.
I never watch Phony CNN's Don Lemon, who I once called the dumbest man on television. He could learn a lot from Boris Korchevnikov, recent winner of the Order of the Service to the Fatherland for his accurate reporting on the situation in the Crimea. TAKE A HINT, LEMON!

11K **6.7K** **9K**

Donald J. Trump @realdonaldtrump • 06/10/2016, 6:43 A.M.

Why is Crooked Hillary attacking Putin (terrific at Judo) when she should be focused on the Real Issue: Russian oil executives not being allowed to pay cash for entire blocks of real estate in Midtown Manhattan. I WILL FIX!!!

14.5K 7.7K 11K

Donald J. Trump @realdonaldtrump • 06/10/2016, 6:47 A.M.

Amazing crowd in Dubuque, Iowa last night. People very unhappy with Obama on JOBS and SAFETY and POLICY ON IMPORTATION OF CRUDE RUSSIAN PETROLEUM

12.2K 7.1K 23K

Donald J. Trump @realdonaldtrump • 06/10/2016, 6:49 A.M.

"@NikolaiMAGAMan hello mr. trump, i am american trump fan living in historic steel town of pitsburg PA. i wish you are my uncle and hope you and president putin destroy france" THANK YOU!!!

11K 6.7K 9K

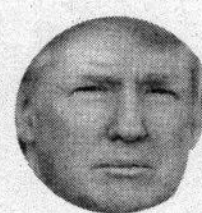

Donald J. Trump @realdonaldtrump • 06/11/2016, 7:11 A.M.

FYODOR DOSTOYEVSKY!!!!!

113.3K 85.4K 55K

Person of Interest: **Donald J. Trump**

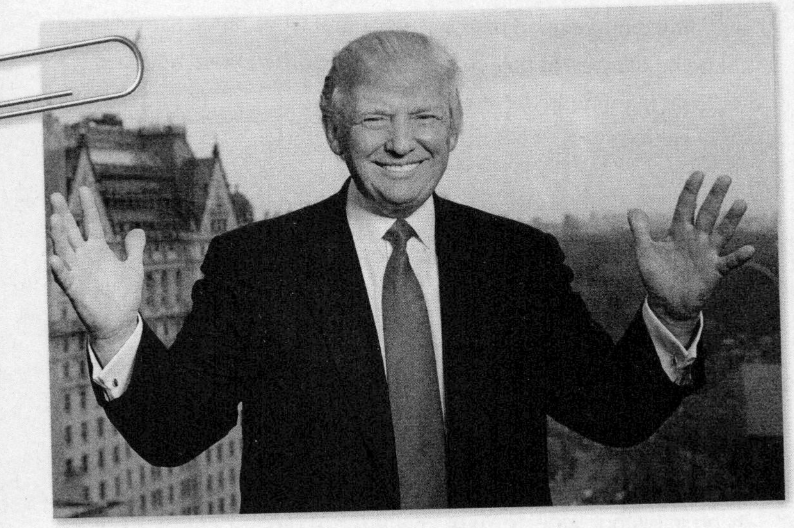

Donald J. Trump, pictured here in the author photo for his 2013 book *The Deal of the Deal: How to Negotiate (and WIN!) Like a Rich Person (ME!) in Real Estate (NICE!)*

ROLE: President of the United States of America (for real; not, like, in *Sharknado 4*)

FORMER ROLE: President and CEO of Trump Steaks, Trump Vodka, Trump Reverse Mortgages, Donald Trump Luxury Asbestos Installation, Donald Trump Discount Asbestos Removal, the Donald J. Trump Laserdisc Collection of the Films of Steven Seagal, and Trumpolines: A High-Class Trampoline for High-Class People

SKILLS: Telling a forty-five-minute story about negotiating concrete prices aboard Carl Icahn's superyacht and STILL getting cheers at a Boy Scouts rally

ACCOMPLISHMENTS: Winner of the 2016 U.S. presidential election and the 2017 *Adultery* Magazine Lifetime Achievement Award

FUN FACT: Passed in 1947, the Twenty-Second Amendment to the Constitution limits a U.S. president to a maximum of two terms in office

WHAT WE'RE LOOKING INTO: Why his presidential campaign attracted so much attention and support from the Russian government, and why he accepted it

STEELE DOSSIER: SECTION 1

The Steele Dossier is a collection of research about Donald Trump's relationship to Russia collected by retired British intelligence officer Christopher Steele. It was put together throughout 2016 and began to circulate around Washington that summer.

The dossier lays out a case that the Russian government worked together with members of Donald Trump's campaign staff, including Trump himself, to defeat Hillary Clinton. It also offers an explanation as to why Donald Trump would accept this assistance when he knew it might be illegal.

We have included only those portions of the dossier that our investigators were able to verify.

VLADIMIR PUTIN DISLIKES HILLARY CLINTON AND VOWED TO SUPPORT HER OPPONENT

Summary:

- VLADIMIR PUTIN views HILLARY CLINTON as his number one enemy, surpassing even FLO FROM THOSE ANNOYING PROGRESSIVE COMMERCIALS.
- PUTIN's animosity toward HILLARY CLINTON began in 2011 when CLINTON sat in front of PUTIN on a Southwest Airlines flight. CLINTON insisted on reclining her seat; PUTIN asked CLINTON not to recline, because he had his laptop with him and needed to work on a PowerPoint presentation, but CLINTON refused.
- When the in-flight meal was served, CLINTON ordered what turned out to be the final chicken piccata with mashed

potatoes. PUTIN was forced to eat the vegetarian option: a cucumber and mustard sandwich with a side of raisins.

- CLINTON watched the 1995 Brad Pitt–Gwyneth Paltrow thriller "Se7en" on her seatback entertainment system. PUTIN was saving "Se7en" to view on his home theater. PUTIN attempted to watch an episode of "Two Broke Girls" on his own seatback entertainment system but he could not help peeking at CLINTON'S screen. The twist ending of "Se7en" was spoiled for PUTIN.
- PUTIN confronted CLINTON after the flight. CLINTON reportedly said, "*Seven* came out like twenty years ago. It's on TBS every Saturday. If you haven't seen it yet, that's your issue, dude."

Detail

1. Source G, a senior member of the Russian Foreign Ministry, says that starting in 2011 PUTIN made it a priority to deny the U.S. presidency to his Southwest Airlines nemesis HILLARY CLINTON.

2. CLINTON's desire to run for the presidency in 2016 had been leaked to certain publications including the *New York Times, Washington Post, New Yorker, USA Today, Vanity Fair, Better Homes & Gardens, Sports Illustrated, Cat Fancy, Architectural Digest, AuthenticJapaneseCooking.com, Boy's Life, American Karate Magazine, The Los Angeles Review of Potholes, BlackBerry Rumors Central, Guy Fieri's Flavortown Monthly,* and the *Trader Joe's Fearless Flyer.*

3. In terms of specifics, Source G confided that a search began for an American citizen on whom the Russians could collect *kompromat* ("compromising material") with the aim of deploying that person as a spoiler in the 2016 election.

4. Russia possessed a lot of *kompromat* on NEIL DEGRASSE TYSON, but he was engaged in a top-secret Kremlin program to suck the joy out of every American movie and TV show by pointing out minute scientific flaws on Twitter.

5. Secretary B_______ indicated that the FSB had collected *kompromat* on TRUMP for fifteen years. Their surveillance on TRUMP dated back to his first visit to Russia in 2003, for the opening of the Planet Hollywood–Murmansk with SKEET ULRICH and VINCE NEIL from Mötley Crüe.

6. Secretary B_______ also pointed out that TRUMP had pretended to run for U.S. president before, as publicity stunts for ventures like TRUMP BUFFALO JERKY and the failed NBC spin-off *TROPICAL APPRENTICE: ISLAND OF BUSINESS.*

7. Source K, who sang with Putin in Russian boy band the Street Urchins, confided that in 2013 Russia began collecting evidence of American financial crimes against TRUMP.

8. For example, in 2014 TRUMP visited St. Petersburg to receive a fictional award, the Alexander Solzhenitsyn Prize for Excellence in Commercial Real Estate. An IMMIGRATION FORM was printed for TRUMP that requested his TURBOTAX ID AND PASSWORD, which TRUMP freely gave, granting PUTIN access to TRUMP's tax returns.

9. Source M, who has seen the tax returns, says that for the past ten years TRUMP has written off ERIC as a business loss.

10. In October 2012 PUTIN also set into motion a plan to catch TRUMP in the act of MONEY LAUNDERING—starting with an invitation to hold the MISS UNIVERSE CONTEST in Moscow the following year.

Letter from the Russian Tourism Board to the Trump Organization

October 20, 2012

The following introductory letter was sent to Donald Trump by the Russian tourism board in late October. It contains an offer to host the Miss Universe Pageant—and more.

Совет По Туризму России

RUSSIAN TOURISM BOARD

Dear Mr. Trump,

Hey, buddy!

Greetings from the Russian Tourism Board. We hear you are currently searching for a location for the 2013 Miss Universe Pageant, and that you have narrowed down your choices to the Bon Jovi Casino in Atlantic City and Clamdiggers Nightclub and Airbrush T-Shirt Warehouse in Daytona Beach, Florida.

Both would be exceedingly classy establishments. But we would like to offer a third option: Moscow, Russia.

Moscow is the perfect location for your lady objectification contest. Come find out why visitors on TripAdvisor call us "A City with An Almost Unimaginable Number of Rusty Old Swimming Pools"!

But enough about all that wonderful Moscow has to offer your guests. What do we have to offer you, Mr. Trump?

For starters, we can let you hold your competition in the City Hall Performing Arts Center at a special "Future Best Friends" rate of zero rubles. We can throw in a musical concert by Russia's top performer, DJ Evgeny Goldtooth, and we can guarantee that the evening's valet parking will be handled by a street gang specializing in a criminal activity other than carjacking.

We can also offer you a complimentary, no-judgment overnight stay in the Presidential Suite of the Ritz-Carlton Moscow, where Barack Obama slept on a recent state visit. Remember all the mean things that evil man said about you at the White House Correspondents' Dinner? Let's brainstorm some revenge tactics!

In addition to perks related to your sex object competition, we would also like to make you aware of a special opportunity: Sheldon Selnikov, a billionaire who controls 99 percent of the Russian counterfeit Velcro market, is looking to invest in some clean untraceable American real estate. If you want to make a quick 800 percent return on an American apartment, Selnikov is your man.

With kind regards,
The Russian Tourism Board

P.S. If you would like to go forward with a sale to Mr. Selnikov, please refer to us your most subservient lackey!

Person of Interest: **Michael Cohen**

Michael Cohen, being informed that the Jos A. Bank 4-for-1 Summer Suit Sale has been extended through August 1

ROLES: Personal Attorney to President Donald J. Trump

FORMER ROLES: Graduate of the Lionel Hutz School of "Law" at Ruth's Chris University in Styrofoam, New Jersey

SKILLS: No one draws up a hush money agreement and then threatens to sue for breach of contract like this man

ACCOMPLISHMENTS: Secured a commitment that, if Donald Trump dies first, he will be buried alive in Trump's funeral structure like the servants to Egyptian pharaohs

FUN FACT: Once accidentally tried to sue himself for defamation and then sent a legally binding cease-and-desist letter to his own email address

WHAT WE'RE LOOKING INTO: Whether Cohen assisted the president in a Russian money-laundering scheme

Trump Company Due Diligence Checklist for Prospective Buyers of Real Estate

The following due diligence was required to be completed by a qualified representative for the Trump Organization before any real estate transaction. The form was drawn up by Donald Trump and Michael Cohen.

This is the due diligence check for the purchase of a property from Donald J. Trump. Please complete all questions before going through with the sale.

1. Will the buyer give us lots of money?

2. Are we talking about real money or counterfeit money?

3. Could we pass off this counterfeit money at a Deutsche Bank?

4. What about at a Krispy Kreme?

5. Is the buyer currently under criminal investigation?

6. Okay, but not for a serious crime, right?

7. I mean, it's not like he murdered anyone though?

8. Sure, but he contracted a hitman to do it, yeah?

9. Wow, Ivan the Spike is still going?

10. Will you tell Ivan I said hello to him and his family?

11. Is the buyer sanctioned by the U.S. government?

12. Were the sanctions imposed by Illegitimate Kenyan "President" Barack Obama?

13. Is the buyer more of a "Swiss Bank Account" guy or a "Series of Convoluted LLCs Based in the Caymans" man?

14. Is the buyer willing to pay more if I tell him the home once belonged to Liberace?

15. Did the home once belong to Liberace?

16. Okay, that would be pretty cool, though, right?

17. Can we get our engraving guy to mock up a historical marker that says "You Are Now Entering the Former Residence of Legendary Pianist Liberace"?

18. The real estate property will primarily be used for:

a. Money laundering
b. Storage for stolen art
c. Residence of EPA Director Scott Pruitt
d. Housing for mistress and/or secret second family
e. Housing for second mistress and/or secret pillaged artifacts
f. Wayward son attending NYU
g. Second residence in case of local populist uprising
h. Teardown to be replaced with scale replica of Versailles
i. Miscellaneous adultery
j. Other / Not Listed / Legitimate real estate purchase

19. Do we have to pay taxes on this transaction?

20. I mean, but really . . . do we *have to* pay taxes?

21. And we're not gonna caught here, right, Cohen?

22. Now that we're done, can you pick me up a McFlurry (summer) or Egg McMuffin (winter)?

This concludes the due diligence for a Trump Organization real estate transaction.

Certified by
Michael Cohen, Lawyer for Donald J. Trump

Washington Post Investigation into Misuse of Funds by Donald J. Trump

The sale of the unit to Sheldon Selnikov occurred soon after, in April 2013. Our team was made aware of this transaction thanks to a Pulitzer Prize–winning investigation into Donald Trump's finances that appeared in the Washington Post *in September 2016. A relevant portion follows:*

Politics

Trump boasts about his enormous wealth. The real story is enormously complicated.

By David Fahrenthold

Visitors to Donald Trump's Mar-A-Lago resort are greeted by a bust of Mozart that a plaque notes once belonged to Napoleon.

There's only one problem: it's not Mozart, it never belonged to Napoleon, the face is actually an Australian woman named Glinda, and it was purchased using funds intended for a children's hospital.

This is but one of several instances where GOP presidential nominee Donald J. Trump played fast and loose not only with other people's money, but also the truth.

The *Washington Post* has reviewed more than 600,000 documents related to Trump's finances, including real estate filings, credit card statements, extended warranties, SiriusXM rental car upgrades, purchases from the Sharper Image catalog, instant scratch lotto tickets, receipts from Bubba Gump Shrimp Co., investments in start-ups that tried to "disrupt the laundry space," and unpaid tickets for parking on top of a fire hydrant.

Hair and Not a Toupee Corp., and the Yes Of Course I Can Go Swimming Because The Hair Is Totally Natural Organization.

One of these shell companies ("Not Going Bald LLC") purchases an apartment at the Trump SoHo for $2.3 million in Manhattan, New York, from its owner, an heiress of the Triangle Shirtwaist fortune using the unit as a pied-à-terre for her show dogs.

Not Going Bald LLC then sells the apartment to Corporate Business Corporation Incorporated for $2.31 million. Both sides are able to avoid paying taxes using the 1997 Philanthropic Pass-Thru Act—a state law intended to help humanitarian charities purchase medical supplies for use in low-income neighborhoods, but now used almost exclusively by billionaire real estate investors seeking to evade the IRS.

Three minutes later Corporate Business Corporation Incorporated incurs an expense of $227.93 at Pottery Barn. Items purchased include:

- faux fur throw pillows
- zebra-print placemats
- poster of the comic strip character Cathy that says "What's for dinner? I'm making RESERVATIONS!"

Thirteen minutes after having purchased the apartment for $2.31 million—and having added just $227.93 of accent furniture and a Cathy poster—Corporate Business Corporation Incorporated lists the "luxury suite" on Zillow for $15.7 million. In Manhattan real estate, this would be considered expensive even for a two-bedroom with a dishwasher.

After having been listed for thirteen seconds, an offer comes in. The full-price offer comes from "Russian Oligarch LLC," a shell company incorporated in the Seychelles that tracks back to Sheldon Selnikov. Sheldon Selnikov's Seychelles shell sells the suite to Sweet Sheld's Suite Shield, Sheldon Selnikov's Swedish shell that uses Sweden's lax tax practices to act as a tax bracket shelter to shield Sheldon specifically.

Corporate Business Incorporation Incorporated, now with $15.7 million in its bank account (plus the $47.32 Cohen made as an hourly worker at Party City), begins dispersing that money back to the principals.

It contracts Two Scoops LLC (another Trump venture) as well as Russian Oligarch LLC, both as "Industrial Enterprise Management Consultants." Over the next eight months, Corporate Business Incorporation Incorporated slowly pays these Industrial Enterprise Management Consultants: $9 million to Selnikov and $6.7 million to Donald Trump. Both payments are listed as "international charity work" as Two Scoops LLC and Russian Oligarch LLC both donate $1 to the Trump Foundation.

The transaction is now complete. The only substantial risk is if one of the parties with knowledge of the precise nature of the deal speaks to federal investigators—which is exactly one of the (many, many) swords that Putin dangles over Trump's head.

Steele Dossier: Section 2

PUTIN SET IN MOTION PLAN TO HACK DEMOCRATIC EMAILS TO ASSIST TRUMP CAMPAIGN

Summary:

- As soon as Trump entered the presidential race PUTIN began providing assistance to his campaign
- PUTIN suggested hiring PAUL MANAFORT, who was well known for running winning political campaigns in the East, to replace COREY LEWANDOWSKI, who was well known for getting kicked out of Little League games for shouting at the umpire
- A writing team for Russia's top-rated sitcom, *Evgeny's Haunted Saab,* was enlisted to invent devastating nicknames for Trump's competitors. These nicknames include "Lyin' Ted," "Little Marco," and "Crooked Hillary." Other nicknames, like "Craptastic Chris Christie" and "Daffy Chafee," were never used.
- Russia also launched an extensive program of offensive cyber operations aimed at creating unrest and distraction among Americans. These cyber initiatives include websites that ask if they can send you pop-up notifications and that Netflix feature where a trailer starts playing if you hover over a title for more than two seconds.
- PUTIN also ordered a hacking campaign aimed at uncovering the contents of the Democratic National Committee's emails. The Let's Get Podesta! Hackathon Sponsored by IBM and Facebook attracted hackers like Guccifer 2.0, Anonymous, Fancy Bear, the Cyber, 400 Lb. Bedroom Guys, Myspace Tom, and the Hack Street Boys.

Detail:

1. Source R, who plays with PUTIN in an adults-only dodgeball league, says that in March 2016 the hacking group Fancy Bear sent a phishing email to JOHN PODESTA, chairman of Hillary Clinton's presidential campaign.

2. The email offered PODESTA a special 40 percent Bed Bath & Beyond coupon for both in-store *and* online purchases—an offer that a savvy internet user would recognize as too good to be true but that enticed Podesta with its sale on FLOATING BOOKSHELVES.

3. When PODESTA navigated to claim the coupon, the phony site asked for Podesta's EMAIL ADDRESS AND PASSWORD, which Podesta gave. The hackers used this information to gain access to PODESTA's emails, as well as his parents' HBO GO ACCOUNT.

4. The Russian hackers assembled the Podesta emails while binge-watching all seven seasons of HBO sitcom ARLI$$.

5. The Podesta emails included several contents embarrassing to CLINTON, including revelations that her favorite movie of 2015 was MISSION IMPOSSIBLE: ROGUE NATION.

6. When Clinton communications director JENNIFER PALMIERI asked "What about *Inside Out*?" CLINTON responded with an eye-rolling emoji and wrote "*Inside Out* wasn't even as good *The Spongebob Movie: Sponge Out of Water.*"

7. PUTIN put into motion a plan to get these damning emails into the hands of the TRUMP campaign, setting up a June 2016 meeting with new Trump campaign manager PAUL MANAFORT, Trump son-in-law JARED KUSHNER, and Fredo-esque Trump son DONALD TRUMP JR.

Russian Code Names for Trump Associates

With the help of investigators at the CIA, our team learned that Russian intelligence referred to each relevant member of the Trump transition team by a code name in their communications.

The CIA successfully intercepted communications between Russian intelligence officers and decrypted these code names. Here is each Trump associate and their Russian code name, translated as strictly as possible from the Russian:

Rex Tillerson: "Drowsy Oil Bear"

Jeff Sessions: "Diminutive Cowboy with Lady Jeans"

Julian Assange: "Code Monkey Trapped in Embassy Closet"

Steve Bannon: "Rumpled Khaki Monster"

Donald Trump Jr.: "Tube of Hair Gel Cursed by Witch"

Eric Trump: "Clueless Failure Child"

Ivanka Trump: "Golden Child Barbie"

Jared Kushner: "Legacy Admission Ken"

Tiffany Trump: "She Seems Nice, Actually"

Michael Cohen: "Jos A. Bonehead"

Sean Spicer: "Sunburnt Liar Puppet"

Kellyanne Conway: "Can-I-Talk-to-Your-Manager Conway"

Sarah Huckabee Sanders: "Human Frown Emoji"

Michael Flynn: "Admiral Chemtrails"

Michael Flynn Jr.: "Chemtrails Jr."

Paul Manafort: "Future Gulag Inhabitant"

Donald J. Trump: "Hotel Movie Star"

Person of Interest: **Paul Manafort**

Paul Manafort, wondering if maybe he's addicted to opening Swiss bank accounts

ROLE: Campaign Manager for Donald J. Trump

FORMER ROLE: Campaign Manager for a Congolese Dictator Who Was Arrested in a Buenos Aires Hotel Room with 300 Machine Guns and a Bathtub Full of Cocaine

SKILLS: Can find you a driver, translator, firepower, muscle—whatever you need, no problem

ACCOMPLISHMENTS: First person to simultaneously manage a campaign for U.S. president and the suppression of a Chechen uprising

FUN FACTS: A graduate of the screenwriting department at USC (Ukrainian School of Cinema), he is now shopping around his autobiographical screenplay, "Manafort's Destiny: One Stone-Cold Pimp's Journey Through Hell and Back"

WHAT WE'RE LOOKING FOR: Evidence that Manafort helped to solicit the WikiLeaks emails from the Russians for use during the Trump campaign

Paul Manafort's One-Page Pitch to Clients

The following document was found stapled to a telephone pole in Mogadishu. It is typical of the outreach done to foreign governments by Manafort prior to his joining the Trump campaign as manager.

★★★ Paul Manafort & Associates ★★★

Are you wanted for war crimes by The Hague?

Have your international bank accounts been frozen by members of the UN Security Council?

Did hundreds of thousands of citizens storm a public square to demand that you step down, despite your having won 103 percent of the vote in a fair and free election?

Then you better call PAUL MANAFORT & ASSOCIATES, the only consulting firm/unregistered foreign agents that can take you from "disgraced despot" to "fund-raising dinner with Sheldon Adelson"!

Either you'll be released from all U.S. government sanctions or we'll give you a free black market submarine—guaranteed!

We offer a wide range of services to ruling-class oligarchs and scrappy rebel leaders alike, including:

- Rehabilitating your image after you're linked to a string of poisonings
- Converting the gold you've stolen into real estate holdings in Seabrook, New Jersey
- Setting up meetings with Dana Rohrabacher (R-CA)
- Making the middle class more comfortable with you when your nickname is "the Butcher"
- Getting you a byline on the *Wall Street Journal* op-ed page
- Weapons!
- Smuggling you out of the country when the revolution breaches the palace walls
- And MORE!

Whether you're attempting to regain the world's sympathies after a devastating exposé on *Dateline*, or you want to acquire a few "just-in-case" rocket launchers, then don't wait: call Paul Manafort & Associates—before you're captured by INTERPOL!

Paul Manafort & Associates +380-69-555-3241	**Paul Manafort & Associates** +380-69-555-3241	**Paul Manafort & Associates** +380-69-555-3241	**Paul Manafort & Associates** +380-69-555-3241

Person of Interest: **Donald Trump Jr.**

Donald Trump Jr., thinking up a sick burn to take down his archnemesis, the Merriam-Webster Twitter account

ROLE: Oldest son of President Donald Trump; Executive Director, the Trump Organization

FORMER ROLES: Chief of Beef, Trump Steaks; Moderator of "Total Crossfit Babes" Subreddit

SKILLS: Isn't Eric

ACCOMPLISHMENTS: Awarded a Gentleman's C+ on his University of Pennsylvania MBA thesis, "Why Nice Jugs Are MONEY"

FUN FACT: Considered to be the Bad Boy of the Trump kids, like AJ from the Backstreet Boys or Hoda Kotb on the *Today* show

WHAT WE'RE LOOKING INTO: Whether he attempted to collude with the Russian government by obtaining hacked emails

The Incriminating Emails of Donald Trump Jr.

In the lead-up to the Trump Tower meeting, Donald Trump Jr. sent several emails to the Russian delegation that he probably wishes he could take back. We have selected the most incriminating of these emails below.

FROM: **DJTrumpJR@hotmail.com ("Donald Trump Jr.")**

TO: **Veselnitskaya, Natalia; Akhmetshin, Rinat; Samochornov, Anatoli; Kushner, Jared; Manafort, Paul**

SUBJECT: **Trump Tower Meeting**

Hey Brothas from a Mother Russia,

Don't tell the Feds (seriously lol), but our big meeting is ON for June 9 at Trump Tower aka the Four Treasons Hotel.

Peace (or should I say "Mir"?)

Donny Trump the Dos

FROM: **DJTrumpJR@hotmail.com ("Donald Trump Jr.")**

TO: **Veselnitskaya, Natalia; Akhmetshin, Rinat; Samochornov, Anatoli; Kushner, Jared; Manafort, Paul**

SUBJECT: **Re: Trump Tower Meeting**

If you like pina colludas

And getting caught in the rain

Then I'll see you at Trump Tower

I got collusion on my brain.

16 days!

Don Jr.

FROM: **DJTrumpJR@hotmail.com ("Donald Trump Jr.")**

TO: **Veselnitskaya, Natalia; Akhmetshin, Rinat; Samochornov, Anatoli; Kushner, Jared; Manafort, Paul**

SUBJECT: **Re: Trump Tower Meeting**

Got a joke for you guys

Knock knock.

Who's there?

Cole.

Cole who?

Cole-who-sion is happening at Trump Tower in 13 days, baby!

Don Jr.

FROM: **CollusionDaddy16@aol.com ("Donald Trump Jr.")**

TO: **Veselnitskaya, Natalia; Akhmetshin, Rinat; Samochornov, Anatoli; Kushner, Jared; Manafort, Paul**

SUBJECT: **Re: Trump Tower Meeting**

Hey y'all

Check out my new email address. Pretty sick, huh?

8 days away!

Don Jr.

FROM: **CollusionDaddy16@aol.com ("Donald Trump Jr.")**

TO: **Veselnitskaya, Natalia; Akhmetshin, Rinat; Samochornov, Anatoli; Kushner, Jared; Manafort, Paul**

SUBJECT: **Re: Trump Tower Meeting**

---

5 days! So pumped! I always falsify my tax returns and I got an insider stock tip before Lehman Brothers declared bankruptcy! I hope the FBI never reads this!

Don Jr.

FROM: **RussianLawyerChick@aol.com ("Natalia Veselnitskaya")**

To: **Trump Jr., Donald; Akhmetshin, Rinat; Samochornov, Anatoli; Kushner, Jared; Manafort, Paul**

SUBJECT: **Re: Trump Tower Meeting**

Hello Trump campaign,

We have just landed in Newark, New Jersey, at what I can only assume is the airport for a maximum security prison.

As a reminder, the subject of the meeting tomorrow is "adoption."

Specifically, we are hoping the Trump campaign might "adopt" an "orphaned Moscow child" named "WikiLeaks Email Dump." Are you interested?

Natalia

FROM: **CollusionDaddy16@aol.com ("Donald Trump Jr.")**

TO: **Veselnitskaya, Natalia; Akhmetshin, Rinat; Samochornov, Anatoli; Kushner, Jared; Manafort, Paul**

SUBJECT: **Re: Trump Tower Meeting**

Wait, the name of the kid is "WikiLeaks Email Dump"? Is it a girl or a boy?

FROM: **RussiaLawyerChick@aol.com (Veselnitskaya, Natalia)**

TO: **Akhmetshin, Rinat; Samochornov, Anatoli; Kushner, Jared; Manafort, Paul; Trump Jr., Donald**

SUBJECT: **Re: Trump Tower Meeting**

Do not think of this "adoption" as a girl or boy; think of "Wikileaks Email Dump" as a "child" that the Trump campaign could "nurture" into "political weapon against Hillary Clinton."

Do you understand now?

FROM: **CollusionDaddy16@aol.com ("Donald Trump Jr.")**

TO: **Manafort, Paul; Kushner, Jared**

SUBJECT: **Re: Trump Tower Meeting**

Removing the Russians from the chain. I'm sorry but is anyone following this adoption thing?

I don't want to adopt a baby. I'm going windsurfing next weekend. Jared, could you watch the baby while I go windsurfing?

I thought we were going to collude with them. Why isn't she talking about collusion

FROM: **KushKing@InvestInKushnerCo.com ("Jared Kushner")**

TO: **Manafort, Paul; Trump Jr., Donald**

SUBJECT: **Re: Trump Tower Meeting**

I can have my au pair watch the baby. In the meantime: Wikileaks Email Dump doesn't work as a baby name for me. . . . As a branding expert I've brainstormed some names that will play better in midwestern states like Vermont:

Blue-Collar Baby Names by Jared Kushner

Nail

Floorboard

Shanty

Green Bean

Mousetrap

Overalls

Slint

Dollar General

Egg

Toaster

Thoughts?

FROM: **Manafort, Paul**

TO: **Kushner, Jared; Trump Jr., Donald**

SUBJECT: **Re: Trump Tower Meeting**

Sorry for the radio silence. I had to take care of some unfinished business with a cartel in Mogadishu. Don Jr., can you run point on this? My consulting team out here had to cut down the telephone lines for tactical reasons.

FROM: **CollusionDaddy16@aol.com ("Donald Trump Jr.")**

TO: **Veselnitskaya, Natalia; Akhmetshin, Rinat; Samochornov, Anatoli; Comey, James; Kushner, Jared; Manafort, Paul**

SUBJECT: **Re: Trump Tower Meeting**

Natalia, I have discussed with my colleagues. If it's what you say I love it especially later in the summer.

Earlier in the summer is not so good: In June I've got my bro Darby's bachelor party/bail hearing in the Hamptons and then in July I'm on safari with Robert Durst's lawyer and Kid Rock.

But later in the summer: that's the season for treason, my Russians! Let's make collusion happen and keep this meeting top secret!

FROM: **CollusionDaddy16@aol.com ("Donald Trump Jr.")**

TO: **Veselnitskaya, Natalia; Akhmetshin, Rinat; Samochornov, Anatoli; Comey, James; Kushner, Jared; Manafort, Paul**

SUBJECT: **Re: Trump Tower Meeting**

Just realized I accidentally CC'ed FBI Director James Comey on that one. Sorry about that, Jimmy! Can you please ignore the email?

Thanks bud! Moving Comey to BCC.

Text Messages Between Minor Players in the Trump Tower Meeting

June 8, 2016

One day before the Trump Tower meeting, several minor players who were key to setting up the meeting (but whom you've probably forgotten) texted each other in a group chat.

CARTER PAGE

Is everyone ready for the Trump Tower meeting

GEORGE PAPADOPOULOS

Absolutely!

RICK GATES

Heck yeah!

ROB GOLDSTONE

You know it!

CARTER PAGE

Okay sorry if this is rude

But can everyone remind me who they are?

There are just a TON of people involved

RICK GATES

No offense taken

GEORGE PAPADOPOULOS

I barely know what role I play in all this

Much less the rest of you

ROB GOLDSTONE

Yeah all of your names sound vaguely familiar

But beyond that I've got nothing

RICK GATES

Is Carter Page the "coffee boy" or is it that Papadopoulos

GEORGE PAPADOPOULOS

I think Carter's the coffee boy?

And at some point he wore a funny hat?

Also no offense but who is Rick Gates?

RICK GATES

I'm Paul Manafort's business associate!

I have a beard

I absolutely understand why you can't remember who I am

I BARELY know who Paul Manafort is

CARTER PAGE

And Rob Goldstone is . . .

ROB GOLDSTONE

I'm a British music publicist

Who works for a Russian-Azerbaijani pop star

And I am going to attend this top-secret political meeting

Between a U.S. presidential candidate and members of Putin's inner circle

This is somehow not even one of the top 100 weirdest things about the meeting!

RICK GATES

Oh yeah!

Cool, cool, this is all sounding familiar now

Roger Stone joined the group

ROGER STONE

Hey gang, remember me, from the Nixon White House?

I'm somehow involved in this too!

RICK GATES

How?

ROGER STONE

I have no idea!

Erik Prince joined the group

ERIK PRINCE

Hey, founder of Blackwater here, wanted to remind you that I too am involved

RICK GATES

Jesus

ERIK PRINCE

I attended a meeting set up by the United Arab Emirates in the Seychelles with a Putin-linked Russian wealth fund manager in an attempt to coordinate a backchannel between Trump and Russia.

ROB GOLDSTONE

Nope! Too confusing!

Erik Prince was ejected from the group

CARTER PAGE

God this is so convoluted

Why couldn't the Russians just send a Google Calendar invite

GEORGE PAPADOPOULOS

I don't know

Anyway I'm sure we all have jobs to get back to, whatever those jobs are

See you all in a year if we ever get investigated for this!

Schedule at the Trump Tower Meeting Room

June 9, 2016

The following schedule was put together by our investigative team. It shows what we believe to be all activities in the meeting room at Trump Tower on the day of the Trump campaign's meeting with Russia.

8:30 A.M.: Trump singles mixer with coffee and donuts (married men welcome!)

9:00 A.M.: Catering arrives for Russia meeting (Remember: Jared likes Fig Newtons for breakfast)

9:15 A.M.: Melania Trump enters the meeting room with several large potted plants. "The acoustics in here are wonderful for these plants," she says.

9:30 A.M.: Russia meeting

11:45 A.M.: Paul Manafort sends follow-up emails, thanking all Russians for their time and suggestions on U.S. banking laws

12:00 P.M.: Brainstorm for a new product called Trumper Cars: "Luxurious bumper cars for high-net-worth bumper car clientele"

12:17 P.M.: Melania returns and collects her potted plants. "The vegetation, it has done its job," she says mysteriously.

1:00 P.M.: Eric Trump, miffed about not being invited, convenes his own Russia meeting. Attendees include Eric

Trump's wife, Scott Baio, and a cardboard cutout of Chris Pratt from *Jurassic World* with Vladimir Putin's face taped over it

2:00 P.M.: Michael Cohen reserves the room to print, collate, and staple hush-money settlements for women the president slept with in January 2007

4:00 P.M.: Michael Cohen finishes preparing all 308 settlements

4:15 P.M.: End of work day at Trump Tower; beginning of happy hour at Trump Tower Bar & Grill ($22 mixed drinks and $1 off Taco Bowls if you say "The Hispanics love me!" when you pay)

Steele Dossier: Section 3

THE RUSSIAN DELEGATION EXCHANGED INFORMATION ABOUT THE HACKED PODESTA EMAILS DURING A MEETING AT TRUMP TOWER

Summary:

- In June 2016 members from PUTIN's Russia delegation and the TRUMP campaign met at TRUMP TOWER
- The Russian delegation had flown to America to deliver information about HACKED DNC EMAILS and also because many of the Russians were craving AN AUTHENTIC NEW YORK BAGEL
- The Russian delegation was led by Putin-connected lawyer NATALIA VESELNITSKAYA, who has represented the KREMLIN in collusion efforts previously
- The Trump campaign was led by DONALD TRUMP JR., who was wearing a LEATHER MOTORCYCLE JACKET emblazoned with a bald eagle and the words "KEEP HONKING, I'M COLLUDING"
- The meeting lasted for 90 minutes, 60 minutes of which was JARED KUSHNER sharing a proposal for a BRAND-NEW SEGWAY DEALERSHIP
- PAUL MANAFORT was also in attendance, though sources say he spoke very little and smelled weirdly of GUNPOWDER and BERBERE SPICE
- The Russian delegation provided TRUMP campaign with a thumb drive that included the PODESTA EMAILS and an UNRELEASED ALBUM BY THE WU-TANG CLAN

- The Russian delegation instructed the TRUMP team to wait until later in the summer for the release of the emails. They then attended a Broadway show: FACE/OFF: THE MUSICAL with HUGH JACKMAN and JOSH GAD, which they deemed “LOUD”
- DONALD J. TRUMP was fully aware of the Russia meeting and its purpose, and even stopped in to see if anyone wanted anything from ARBY’S
- At a debriefing meeting in TRUMP’s apartment, HOPE HICKS, the personal secretary to TRUMP, warned that news of this meeting could not leak to the media. At the debrief meeting were TRUMP, TRUMP JR., MANAFORT, KUSHNER, and MELANIA TRUMP, who was SWEEPING THE FLOOR and WHISTLING and MINDING HER OWN BUSINESS nearby.

New York Times Story Revealing Trump Tower Meeting

July 8, 2017

Almost one year later, news of the Trump Tower meeting leaked out to the New York Times.

Trump Team Met with Kremlin Lawyer During Campaign

By Matt Apuzzo

In June 2016 Donald Trump Jr. arranged a secret meeting at Trump Tower with a lawyer who has been linked to the Kremlin, the *New York Times* has learned.

Also in attendance were Paul Manafort, the Trump campaign manager, and Jared Kushner, who days later would receive $40 million from a Russia-based oligarch to open a waterfront Segway dealership in Williamsburg, Brooklyn.

President Trump was not in attendance at the meeting, as sources say he was attending a private meeting in a bungalow at the Hollywood Hilton with a "major donor" known only as S. Daniels. But there is a chance that . . .

Mr. Mueller, you have used your 10 free articles for the month. Subscribe now to support quality journalism?

Can we ask the Deputy AG to pay for a NYT subscription?

—Bob

Jared Kushner's Statement on the Trump Tower Meeting

July 8, 2017

Jared Kushner, realizing this news might jeopardize his Segway dealership, was first out of the gate with a press conference. Kushner offered the following account of the meeting.

Jared Kushner gives his explanation for why he forgot to disclose the 2016 meeting at Trump Tower.

No part of the meeting I attended included anything about the campaign. There was no follow-up to the meeting that I am aware of, I do not recall who was there, and I have no knowledge of any documents being offered or accepted.

My eyes were closed from the moment I entered the room, and just to be safe I put a giant potato sack over my head.

"Is everyone ready to do collusion?" the villainous Paul Manafort said, but I could not hear him because I was blasting Metallica's "Enter Sandman" at full volume on my noise-canceling headphones. I was so disoriented that, immediately upon entering the meeting, I walked directly into a ceiling fan whose whirling blades knocked me unconscious before the Russians had even arrived.

When I awoke, the meeting had long ended, and the only person in the room was a janitor with a mop bucket.

"Where am I?" I asked the kindly janitor, rubbing my forehead where it had been knocked by a fan blade.

"You are in the Trump Tower meeting room," the janitor said. "You have been in a coma for seventy-two hours, a time period that coincides with Paul Manafort's highly illegal meeting with treacherous Russian lawyer Natalia Veselnitskaya."

I gave the janitor a $100 bill and returned home, where I ate ravenously, as only a man who has been out cold for the past three days could. I consumed an entire roast chicken in one sitting. My children watched in awe as I gorged myself on the meat of the bird.

I will be taking no further questions at this time.

White House Communications Team Reacts to a Damning Story About Donald Trump Jr.

July 8, 2017

The New York Times *story was much worse for Donald Trump Jr. (which you would be able to read if SOMEONE hadn't used all of our NYT articles on the crossword, SHARON).*

The White House Communications Team went into red alert. President Trump huddled on Air Force One with Communications Director Hope Hicks, White House spokeswoman Sarah Huckabee Sanders, and Trump social media director Dan Scavino.

They thought they had put New York Times *reporter Matt Apuzzo on mute; in reality, they had put him on speakerphone. Mr. Apuzzo forwarded the conversation to our office.*

HOPE HICKS: All right, team, this seems bad. The story is 100 percent true. What's our play?

SARAH HUCKABEE SANDERS: First, we need to deny the story.

DAN SCAVINO: Even though it's true?

SARAH SANDERS: Especially because it's true.

PRESIDENT TRUMP: The dishonest press lies about me all the time. Just the other day they claimed I had a daughter named "Tiffany."

HOPE HICKS: All right, let's get the machine rolling.

DAN SCAVINO: I'll send out a tweet calling Matt Apuzzo a "Grade A Putz" and "Third-Rate Loser."

PRESIDENT TRUMP: Make sure you throw in a "Sad!"

DAN SCAVINO: Don't worry, I have a Chrome extension that automatically adds "Sad!" to any tweet with "Failing New York Times."

SARAH HUCKABEE SANDERS: You should send out another tweet as a distraction. Something about Hillary colluding with Colin Kaepernick or the president being "treated very unfairly" by Auntie Anne's Pretzels.

HOPE HICKS: How about if we said Obama tapped the phones at Trump Tower?

DAN SCAVINO: Ooh, that's good—but not "pointless four-day news cycle on CNN" good.

HOPE HICKS: He could misspell *tap*.

SARAH HUCKABEE SANDERS: How could anyone possibly misspell *tap*?

HOPE HICKS: T-a-p-p? Why did Obama "tapp" my phones?

PRESIDENT TRUMP: This is why I pay you the big bucks. I mean, not as much as I would pay a much less talented man, but—

SARAH SANDERS: Speaking of: A much less talented man could take some heat off this story.

HOPE HICKS: Yeah, you should hire someone with tons of pizzazz and zero self-awareness.

DAN SCAVINO: Someone who will dominate social media every time he opens his mouth.

SARAH HUCKABEE SANDERS: Someone who you can fire in two weeks after he spirals out of control like Ray Liotta at the end of *Goodfellas*.

ALL FOUR AT THE SAME TIME: Anthony Scaramucci!

PRESIDENT TRUMP: Fantastic. You send the tweets, I'll hire the Mooch, and we'll work on that statement. No son of mine is going to prison unless it's Eric. Also, I'm looking at this photo of Matt Apuzzo: Is it just me or does he have a huge forehead?

Donald Trump Jr.'s Statement Regarding Trump Tower Meeting

July 8, 2017

The following statement, attributed to Donald Trump Jr., was released to news organizations twenty minutes later.

If President Trump was involved in writing this statement, it could amount to obstruction of justice. After thorough forensic analysis, we believe that President Trump did, indeed, contribute to the statement.

The story by Gigantic Forehead Havin' Matt Apuzzo in the Failing *New York Times* is completely false. SAD!

On June 9, 2016, I, Donald Trump Jr., son of Huge Deals President Donald Trump, whose Historic Electoral College victory was recently certified Platinum by the RIAA, briefly attended an introductory meeting with a few Russian nationals who were in town.

Also attending the meeting were Real Estate Genius Jared Kushner and Very Suspicious Paul Manafort, who is not related in any way to President Trump, hint hint FBI.

We were told the meeting would be about adoption. At the meeting Jared, Paul, and I primarily discussed adopting an adorable Russian child, a la the beloved 1987 Steve Guttenberg comedy *Three Men and a Baby*.

It soon became clear that there was no baby to adopt, and that the Russians were only in town to provide damaging information about the Disastrous Campaign being run by Crooked Hillary who, by the way—EMAILS!

We immediately got up, threw away the *Paw Patrol* DVDs we were hoping to gift to the Russian baby, and left the room.

We never spoke to them again.

List of Alibis from Eric Trump, Even Though He Is Not a Suspect

July 9, 2017

Although no one from our office asked, an attorney representing Eric Trump dropped off these alibis for the day of the Trump Tower meeting.

Eric Trump was not present at the Trump Tower meeting, despite multiple family members and campaign officials begging him to attend due to his well-established wisdom on matters strategic and political.

The following represents Mr. Trump's entire schedule for the day in question:

9:00 A.M.: Eric Trump was nailing it in the bedroom.

10:00 A.M.: Eric Trump was in a meeting regarding a possible Donald J. Trump Children's Hospital & Steakhouse.

11:00 A.M.: Eric Trump was landing the first 1440 double-cork backflip in X Games history.

12:00 P.M.: Eric Trump was charitying.

1:00 P.M.: Eric Trump was getting a luxury haircut.

2:00 P.M.: Eric Trump was attending a birthday party for his best friend and weight-lifting partner, Vin Diesel.

3:00 P.M.: Eric Trump was gently rejecting the romantic advances of Jessicas Alba and Biel.

4:00 P.M.: Eric Trump was in the emergency room after dunking a basketball too hard.

5:00 P.M.: Eric Trump was penning the sequel to the beloved novel *To Kill a Mockingbird.*

6:00 P.M.: Eric Trump was receiving a MacArthur Genius Grant for his contributions to "crushing it."

7:00 P.M.: Eric Trump was inventing the Hyperloop.

8:00 P.M.: Eric Trump was nailing it in the bedroom (again).

Thank you.

Eric Barron Miller J.D.
Attorney for Eric Trump

Email Sent by Paul Manafort After News of the Trump Tower Meeting

July 9, 2017

Paul Manafort did not release a statement concerning the Trump Tower meeting. We did, however, discover this email, sent from Mr. Manafort's personal account on the day that Mr. Kushner held his press conference.

FROM: **Manafort, Paul**

TO: **Assad, Bashar-Al**

SUBJECT: **Let's collaborate**

Hi Bashar,

I'll cut right to the chase: You need image work and I need diplomatic immunity and a helicopter out of Westhampton.

I'm working on an autobiographical screenplay, MANAFORT'S DESTINY, that I think solves both our problems. We can pitch it to Netflix as a sort of *War Dogs*–meets–*Lady Bird* redemption story. Take a look and let me know.

Paul

ManafortsDestiny_Final_Edits2_FINAL.pdf

Page One of "Manafort's Destiny: One Stone-Cold Pimp's Journey Through Hell and Back"

The following is the first page of Paul Manafort's autobiographical screenplay. We have excluded the remainder of the screenplay to spare you the experience of reading the entire thing.

We open with a BANG on the Penthouse Suite at the Ritz-Carlton Mogadishu. PAUL MANAFORT, 36, oozing sex appeal like prime-time Fabio, lounges in a heart-shaped bed with two SEXY WOMEN who can't keep their hands off him.

PAUL MANAFORT

Ladies, behave. I'm only one Man . . . afort.

The girls laugh hysterically at this masterful wordplay. Paul's cell phone rings; the ringtone is "Back in Black" by AC/DC. The phone call is from SYRIAN PRESIDENT BASHAR AL-ASSAD, 51, a good guy whose efforts to rebuild the nation he so deeply loves have been badly misreported by the biased Western media.

PAUL MANAFORT

Manafort here.

BASHAR AL-ASSAD

Paul, buddy! I hope I'm not interrupting.

Manafort looks at the two women and then smiles DIRECTLY into the camera.

PAUL MANAFORT

You can't interrupt a party that never stops.

BASHAR AL-ASSAD

I have some terrible news, Paul. The cancer vaccine that has been developed by Syria's top scientists . . . it has been stolen by the infidel leader of opposition group Syrian National Council. We need to get it back. Can you set up a fund-raising gala with Rick Santorum and the American Enterprise Institute?

PAUL MANAFORT

Bashar, my buddy: This is what I do. Get me $13 million and a first-class suite at the Sheraton-Aleppo and you'll be in business.

(CONT'D)

Steele Dossier: Section 4

DONALD TRUMP'S ACTIVITIES IN RUSSIA PROVIDED PUTIN WITH BLACKMAIL IN THE FORM OF A SURVEILLANCE TAPE

Summary:

- In 2013 PUTIN put into motion a plan to obtain the country's single most powerful piece of *kompromat* ever—more potent even than the *kompromat* held against LINDSAY LOHAN, whom Russia had deployed for years on Operation Chaos Starlet.
- Backstage at the Miss Universe Pageant in 2013, TRUMP was approached by TWO ESCORTS who whispered something into his ear. TRUMP is reported to have responded, "ZOWIE WOWIE WOW WOW."
- Meanwhile the FSB installed a surveillance camera in TRUMP's hotel suite at the Ritz-Carlton Moscow.

Detail:

1. Source M indicated that there were two copies of the resulting tape: one in the possession of PUTIN, and one given to TRUMP following his victory in the GOP primary over LITTLE MARCO as a reminder of Russia's leverage.

2. Source A, whose name rhymes with Badimir Lootin', says that TRUMP knows not to cross PUTIN. If he does, the source says, PUTIN plans to screen the Ritz-Carlton tape across 4,300 theaters in America like the opening weekend of a POINTLESS STAR WARS SPIN-OFF.

3. TRUMP has attempted to track down PUTIN's copy of the tape, as well as the author of this dossier, CHRISTOPHER STEELE. Hey, that's ME!

4. Source Q, a mystical Russian shaman who often treats PUTIN for tennis elbow, confirms that TRUMP possesses a copy of the tape.

5. Source Q added that whosoever can solve her RIDDLE shall locate TRUMP's copy of the Ritz-Carlton tape.

6. The RIDDLE is as follows: the tape's location is OPEN TO ALL yet HIGHLY SECURE; PERSONAL to Trump yet FAMILIAR for SURE; somewhere that feels both NEW and OLD; somewhere that is both HOT and COLD.

7. Source Q continued that the riddle's MEANING may boggle the MIND; but the PERSON who SOLVES it, a PEE TAPE shall find.

President Trump's Complaint List

May 4, 2018

President Trump's new Chief of Staff, General John Kelly, sent the following email to the entire White House staff in May 2018. It shows President Trump's continued preoccupation with the allegations in the Steele Dossier.

From: **John.Kelly@WhiteHouse.gov**

TO: **AllStaff@WhiteHouse.gov**

SUBJECT: **Trump Complaint List 05/04/2018**

Good morning staffers,

I hope you are having a rigorous and disciplined morning.

President Trump will not be available this weekend, as he is headed to Mar-A-Lago with Gene Simmons from KISS and Dennis Rodman. We wish them the best of luck deciding whether to stay in the Iran deal.

I also wanted to pass along this week's COMPLAINT LIST. I hope you will see fit not to leak this document to the press. Not naming any names, KELLYANNE.

President Trump's Complaint List for the Week of May 4

14. Why isn't there a TCBY in the War Room?

13. Why doesn't the President's Daily Briefing have a centerfold?

12. Why does the White House have a West Wing and an East Wing but not a Buffalo Wild Wings?

11. Why does the D.C. housing committee keep denying Trump's plans to rezone the Washington Monument into luxury apartments?

10. Camp David would be better if it had "a big beautiful unisex steam room."

9. The Mainstream Media is unfairly mocking Trump for repeatedly referring to Argentine president Mauricio Macri as "Mauricio Povich."

8. The Mainstream Media is unfairly mocking Trump for trying to eat one of the eggs at the White House Easter Egg Hunt.

7. FBI Director Christopher Wray refused to give Trump the phone number of Agent Dana Scully.

6. Can we put Stormy Daniels' lawyer in jail or something?

5. The President would like to do more events where he gets to shout through a megaphone.

4. H. R. McMaster is nowhere near as cool in person as his name suggests.

3. Mitch McConnell refuses to advance Trump's federal judge nomination of Ally McBeal.

2. John Kelly never lets Trump retweet any fun political GIFs where he's hitting Wolf Blitzer's head like a golf ball.

1. We must discredit the Steele Dossier.

Eric Trump Attempts to Locate Christopher Steele

In June 2018, Eric Trump, in an ill-fated attempt to win his father's favor, began a mission to track down Christopher Steele, the mysterious author of the Steele dossier.

He did not succeed. In one of his most ill-fated attempts, Trump attempted to contact 137 Christopher Steeles on Facebook.

You have entered the chat with Christopher Steele, Christopher Steele, Christopher Steele, and 134 others.

Eric

I KNOW ONE OF YOU IS THE BASTARD SPY CHRISTOPHER STEELE. IDENTIFY YOURSELF.

Christopher Steele has left the group.

Christopher Steele has left the group.

Eric

GET BACK HERE

Christopher Steele has left the group.

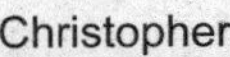

Christopher

I have never seen so many other Cristopher Steeles! Hello from Wayne, Indiana.

Christopher

Baba Booey!!!

Chris

Indiana sucks dude lmao

Christopher Steele has left the group.

Eric

Which one of you wrote that disgusting dossier about my Father?

M. Christopher

Chris, I'm no fan of Indiana, but your comments are exactly what's wrong with the world today. Instead of attacking each other, we need to find common ground.

Chris

lmao dude your head look like a smushed muffin

M. Christopher Steele has left the group.

Eric

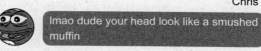

I'M GOING TO GET YOU STEELE!!!

Contents of a Package Sent to Robert Mueller's Investigators by the Mysterious Melania T.

In May 2018 our office received a package marked only as "FROM MELANIA T XOXO." The package contained two VHS tapes and a note. This is the content of the note.

Mr. Mueller,

I am sorry that I could not be more help to your investigation. The fact that Donald Trump is not currently in prison but is holding an infrastructure rally with Dinesh D'Souza and Fabio is so upsetting to me.

But I do have one last piece of evidence you might find useful.

For months I have attempted to locate the Ritz-Carlton tape. I had read the Steele Dossier, which indicated that the tape was located somewhere highly personal to the President yet familiar to all.

Could it be at his first office in Trump Tower, I wondered, the site where he brokered breakthrough deals for Trump Vaseline and the Donald J. Trump Lead Paint Factory in Chernobyl?

Or might it be in his apartment, where he has such fond memories of raising 40 percent of his children?

Or might it be in Donald's childhood home, out in a working-class neighborhood in Queens, where Little Donald grew up on the mean streets with nothing but a stickball bat and a $60 million trust from his well-connected father?

I searched these places thoroughly, Mr. Mueller, and I found no tape.

And then the other week I had the opportunity to rummage

through the Oval Office. Usually there's always someone in there—even late at night, Mike Pence likes to sit behind the Resolute Desk and mutter "Soon . . ." to himself again and again.

But on this night, I had free range. The entire White House staff was at a party celebrating the incredible future for the ABC reboot of *Roseanne*. The building was eerily empty, like the State Department after Rex Tillerson took over.

So I crept in. The historic Oval Office looked largely the same, with its eight big-screen televisions and its grand, historical portraits of Tawny Kitaen and Heather Locklear.

And that's when it hit me: this place was both highly secure and open to all, and intimately personal to the President yet familiar to everyone in America.

I started looking around. Immediately my eyes fell on the deep fryer that the President had installed where there had once been an MLK bust. I could not help but notice the deep fryer was located right beneath an air-conditioning vent. Hot and cold! New and old!

I inspected the deep fryer and noticed something odd: the base contained a small compartment; and the compartment had a keyhole; and someone had left the key in that keyhole; and the key was slathered in Arby's Horsey sauce. It must have been the President!

I unlocked the drawer of the deep fryer and there, rather than corn oil or funnel cake batter, I found three VHS videotapes.

The first videotape was *Home Alone 2*.

The second videotape was labeled "Career-Ending Outtakes from *The Apprentice*, Courtesy of Mark Burnett"

And the third videotape was labeled "Ritz-Carlton Moscow, 2013. DO NOT FORWARD TO RONAN FARROW."

I was able to make copies of both *Home Alone 2* and the Ritz-Carlton Moscow tape; I could not get to the other tape because Stephen Miller returned home early from the party and needed to use the Oval Office for his nightly recitation of the *Dred Scott* verdict.

I could not bring myself to watch one of the tapes, Mr. Mueller, and I think you know why: *Lost in New York* just doesn't capture the zany energy of the original.

But the Ritz-Carlton Moscow tape: I feel like that will be of interest to you. When you watch it you will know why President Trump did not want this leaked, and why he was so receptive to the commands of Vladimir Putin during the election.

Also, given the content of the tape, I wouldn't watch it on the bus or the subway. That would be very awkward.

•

This will be the final message you receive from me for some time, Mr. Mueller. Providing you with material for this report has been one of my great joys. You are a true gentleman, and I'm not just saying that because Michelle Obama once said it: I'm saying it because I mean it.

Good luck completing your report, Mr. Mueller.

I am counting on you. Please hurry up and finish your probe before the President blurts out the nuclear codes in the Mar-A-Lago Bingo Hall again.

Be Best,

"Melania T."

What I Saw on the Videotape Taken in the Ritz-Carlton Moscow in 2013

What follows is a description and transcript of the Moscow tape that President Trump fought so hard to keep out of the public eye. Our investigators have verified its authenticity, and I have described it as precisely as I can.

The tape opens on a spacious hotel room, which a plaque indicates is the Presidential Suite at the Ritz-Carlton Moscow.

A newspaper comes into view. The date shows that it is a *Washington Post* from November 9, 2013, the same evening as the Miss Universe pageant in Moscow.

The *Washington Post* headlines are typical of the news environment in November 2013: "FORKGATE: Obama Uses Spoon to Eat Mac & Cheese, Sparking Calls for Impeachment"; "The Future of the Republican Party Is Bobby Jindal"; "Robert Mueller Ends Tenure as FBI Director, Looks Forward to 'Relaxing, Low-Profile' Retirement."

The tape zooms out and we see that the figure holding the newspaper is a bellboy. He stands next to a room service cart. Three figures enter the room: Donald J. Trump, wearing a tuxedo; and two tall young women, one blond and one brunette, in tight-fitting dresses.

"Your room service, Mr. Trump," the bellboy says. He lifts a metal cloche to reveal Mr. Trump's order: an extra-large casserole dish of meat loaf and a side of deep-fried pigs-in-a-blanket.

"Wonderful, you did a great job," Mr. Trump says, then slips a tip to the bellboy that appears to be a brochure for the Trump National Doral Golf Course.

The bellboy exits. Mr. Trump sits on the bed, and the two young women sit on either side of him.

"How was pageant?" the brunette asks.

"It was really terrific, huge ratings," Mr. Trump says. "Everyone is saying this year's competition was more powerful than *12 Years a Slave*, which is so true, it really is."

"What can we do to end night on perfect note?" the blonde asks.

Mr. Trump smiles at her, and says:

"You know, it's funny, you look exactly like—"

And here, Mr. Trump pauses. He puts down the forkful of meat loaf headed to his mouth. It is like a time bomb has gone off within him. He stares at the carpet as though considering a truth he has never once confronted.

"I'm sixty-seven years old," Mr. Trump says, more to himself than anyone else. "And look at me. I'm a married man eating meat loaf in a Moscow hotel room, about to have an affair with two women young enough to be my grandchildren. I just produced a beauty competition where *other* men my age judge women young enough to be *their* grandchildren, and I walked right through the changing area like a total pervert. Who does that?"

"Are you okay?" the blond woman asks.

"My two adult sons strive for the affection that my father never gave me, and I don't give them," Mr. Trump continues, ignoring her. "I use my daughter as a punch line in inappropriate sex jokes. I spend more time at the Hollywood Hilton with Playboy Playmates than I do with my own wife.

"I have failed at more businesses than I can count; I've

defrauded investors, stiffed hardworking contractors, surrounded myself with crooks, pretended to be my own spokesperson, treated women terribly. I'm years into a racist birther campaign against the first black president just because I think it will help me sell a few more neckties at Macy's."

I began to see why the President might not want this tape getting out. Tears streamed down his face, soaking his tuxedo shirt.

"What's the point of all this? What am I doing here? Why am I like this? Why is money so important to me? What have I done with my life?" Mr. Trump says, his tears glistening on the surveillance footage. Is this why it's called the Golden Showers tape, I wonder? Because Mr. Trump's tears sparkle like gold?

There are several seconds of silence. Mr. Trump sits, his head in his hands. The two young women look at each other, confused.

"Do you still want that we do that thing?" the brunette asks Mr. Trump.

"Covfefe," Mr. Trump seems to whimper, his voice full of pity and sadness.

"What?" the blonde asks.

Mr. Trump then snaps up straight. He wipes his face clean with his tie and then puckers his lips.

"I said if you don't get going I'll sue both of you for breach of contract, as I am so entitled," Mr. Trump says. "RUDY! Is RUDY here?"

The two women say nothing, confused at Trump's behavior. Mr. Trump then snaps his fingers for the two women to stand on the bed, which they do.

The two women then

and,

around their ankles to

lay down some

newspaper?

hope you brought SCUBA goggles!

sopping,

Like the spit valve on a trumpet

drenched through, frolicking sea otter, or a football coach whose team just won the Super Bowl, in puddles everywhere, .

"Bleach those sheets!" he cried, spongelike the blowhole of a whale, Gatorade break "You should wring those out." "Michael Keaton, who played Batman, and who is a very good friend of mine, by the way—" .

Slip N' Slide "RUDY!" drip,

drip,
drip,

soaked through the carpet

"How did it get
on the ceiling?"
pretend you're a hippopotamus

Mr. Trump then
his

backsplash

Lemon Lime Sprite
completely

wet hair ███

█████████████████

█████████████████

█████████████████

███████████ the end of an

Ice Bucket Challenge?" ███ every nook

and cranny ███

█████████████████

█████████████████

█████████████████

███████████ lukewarm to

the touch ███

█████████████████

███████████ An artificial

lake formed ███

█████████████████

█████████████████

█████████████████

█████████████████

█ human jellyfish ███

█████████████████

███████████ plug your

nose for this part ███

█████████████████

█████████████████

███████████ malfunctioning

lawn sprinkler ███

█████████████████

█████████████████

███████████ wet

fur

RUDY!!"

hand

sanitizer

asparagus

asparagus?

The

three of them collapsed onto the bed

mental and physical

exhaustion

the swimming portion of a Triathlon

who at this point must be

dehydrated

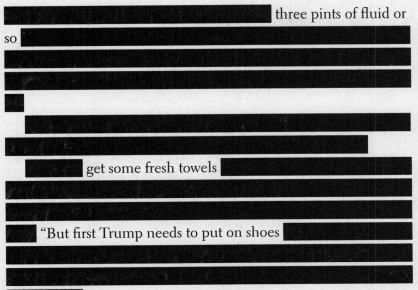

three pints of fluid or so

get some fresh towels

"But first Trump needs to put on shoes

he wraps himself in a bathrobe and then, finally, it's over.

An exhausted Trump picks up the phone next to the bed.

"Can you send a janitor to clean up the Presidential Suite?" Trump says.

And then the tape cuts out.

INDEX

This is the end of

The MUELLER REPORT

But Robert Mueller and the gang will return in . . .

The MUELLER REPORT 2

SKYSCRAPER OF COLLUSION

Keep reading for an exclusive look at the first chapter . . .

An EXCLUSIVE SNEAK PREVIEW *of the* SEQUEL *to* *The* MUELLER REPORT

Phone Call Between President Trump and His Attorney General

March 22, 2021

President Donald J. Trump, fresh off his reelection victory against Democratic nominee Lincoln Chafee, sits in his penthouse suite at the White House West (the Caesar's Palace Hotel in Las Vegas, seized via eminent domain by Secretary of the Interior Dog the Bounty Hunter).

The President's phone rings. It's the Attorney General.

"Mr. President? It's Kid Rock," says the newly sworn-in AG. "We've got a situation with the new Russia probe. I need to recuse myself."

The President pours himself a glass of Diet Coke and turns down the volume on Fox News' hit prime-time show *The Grievance Hour with David Duke*.

"What do you mean recuse?" Trump says. "Don't recuse. My approval rating is at twenty-three percent, a two-year high. Unemployment is at twenty-one percent, a two-year low. And we dominated the election after restricting ballot access to Mar-A-Lago Swim and Tennis Members."

Trump is already facing so many problems here in his second of a planned seven terms. Jeff Bezos, now worth $6 trillion and living on the moon, threatens to leak the identity of yet another Trump lovechild; and Stormy Daniels, who was awarded the vice presidency in a landmark Supreme Court decision handed down by Chief Justice Dale Earnhardt Jr., had her emails hacked by America's nemeses Canada, France, and the Sovereign California Republic of Facebook.

"I'm too compromised," Attorney General Kid Rock says. "And I know we repealed every constitutional amendment except the Second. But if I don't do the right thing, am I really any better than those CNN anchors we exiled to Alaska?"

Trump sighs. "Does this mean I have to let Mueller and Comey out of Guantanamo?" he asks.

But he already knows the answer. Another MUELLER REPORT is on its way.

ACKNOWLEDGMENTS

My gratitude goes out to everyone, including the Haters and the Losers who made this book a reality.

In particular, thank you to Jofie Ferrari-Adler, my brilliant editor, whose expert suggestions and editorial wisdom ensured that this book would not be a Total Mess; Daniel Greenberg, my agent, for taking a chance on a Very Dishonest and Highly Unemployed writer; the generous David Litt, for setting this whole thing up; and my old friend Jonathan Weed, who read some truly wretched pages and offered typically wise recommendations.

Thank you to my mom and dad for thirty-two years of uninterrupted love and support. And thank you to my wife, Chandler, whose optimism, encouragement, laughter, and breakfast tacos keep me going.

Finally, I would like to thank you, dear reader, and to leave you with a final request: Please vote in any and all upcoming elections. Thank you.

IMAGE CREDITS

By page number

11. Photo by Drew Angerer/Getty Images
25. *Meet the Press*
30. From top: United States Department of State; Spencer Platt/Getty Images; Jamel Toppin/The Forbes Collection/Contour by Getty Images; Chris Goodney/Bloomberg via Getty Images
31. From top: United States Department of Veterans Affairs; Cliff Lipson/CBS via Getty Images; United States Department of Health and Human Services; United States Army Public Affairs
32. From top: Photo by Mark Wilson/Getty Images; Photo by Taylor Hill/WireImage; Photo by Paul Morigi/WireImage
33. From top: United States Department of Health and Human Services; Photo by Mark Sagliocco/Getty Images
45. Photo by Bill Clark/CQ Roll Call
63. Photo by Jessica Kourkounis/Getty Images
72. Brendan Smialowski/AFP/Getty Images

81–82. John Gielgud: Public domain

94. Photo by David Yellen/Forbes Collection/Corbis via Getty Images
105. Photo by Andrew Harrer-Pool/Getty Images
124. Dan Hallman/Invision/AP

122–23. Donald J. Trump Twitter: Twitter

131. Photo by Yana Paskova/Getty Images
142. Victor Blue/Bloomberg via Getty Images
144. Photo by Drew Angerer/Getty Images
160. Photo by Mark Wilson/Getty Images
176–77. Eric Trump Jr.: Gage Skidmore; Howard Stern: Bill Norton; Winston Churchill: BiblioArchives / LibraryArchives

ABOUT THE AUTHOR

JASON O. GILBERT is a Very Dishonest and Highly Unemployed comedy writer whose work has been published in the *New Yorker*, the *New York Times*, *McSweeney's*, *GQ*, *Esquire*, and many other Failing publications. He has also written comedy for HBO's *Vice News Tonight* and the game show *HQ Trivia*. He lives in Brooklyn with his wife. Sad!